HOW TO MAKE PUPPETS AND
TEACH PUPPETRY

HOW TO MAKE PUPPETS AND TEACH PUPPETRY

MARGARET BERESFORD
L.G.S.M. (eloc.), Tchs. Cert. N.F.F.
*Cert. Dept. Child Development, University of London
Formerly Headmistress, L.C.C. School*

Illustrations by the author

*Published by Mills & Boon Limited,
50 Grafton Way, Fitzroy Square, London W1*

© *Margaret Beresford 1966*

First published 1966

Second Printing 1968

Printed in the United States of America

*To my husband
who undertook the tedious task
of typing the manuscript*

Contents

		PAGE
AUTHOR'S PREFACE		11

PART ONE: ABOUT PUPPETRY

I	How to Introduce and Teach Puppetry in the Classroom	15
II	Elementary Puppet-making	19
	Simple glove puppet	
	Useful paper puppet	
	Glove puppet with papier mâché head	
	Glove making	
	Costumes	
	Animal puppets from waste material	
	Additional heads	
	Curtains and stages	
	Back-cloths	
	Useful hints	
	Wigs	
	Hands	
III	How to Make Papier Mâché	36
IV	How to Make and Manipulate String Puppets	37
	First string puppet	
	Wooden string puppet	
	Feet for string puppets	
	Legs for string puppets	
	Arms	
	Controls and manipulation	

Contents

		PAGE
V	Shadow Puppetry	49
	How to make shadow puppets	
	Hints on making shadow puppets	
VI	Puppets for Different Age Groups	55
VII	Class Production, and Stories Suitable for Plays	58
VIII	Puppetry Linked to Other Subjects in the Curriculum	63
IX	Short Account of Puppetry in Other Countries	71
	Punch	
	Countries of the Western World	
	Eastern Europe and Asia	

PART TWO:

PUPPET PLAYS WRITTEN AND ACTED BY CHILDREN

X	The Circus Rehearsal	79
XI	The Kitten who Wanted to Purr	88
XII	The Cat who was Lonely	92
XIII	The Three Little Pigs	94
XIV	The Queen of Hearts	100
XV	Mrs. Popple and her Pet Goose	105
XVI	The Nativity	108
XVII	Peter and the Wolf as a Shadow Play	112

List of Diagrams

		PAGE
1.	Puppets for young children	20
2.	Simple paper puppet	21
3.	A paste and paper head	23
5.	Some points in glove-making	24
4.	The making of wigs	26
6.	Puppets from waste material	28
7.	Simple masking and curtains	30
8.	An improvised stage	32
9.	Types of wig	34
10.	Making hands	35
11.	Simple string puppet	38
12.	Wooden string puppet	40
13.	Arms and bodies	41
14.	Joints	43
15.	Proportions for string puppet	44
16.	String puppet stage	46
17.	Controls for string puppets	47
18.	Manipulation	48
19.	Simple shadow screen	51
20.	Chinese type of figure	53
21.	Shadows	54

List of Plates

BETWEEN PAGES 64 AND 65

Spontaneous classroom acting using a small stage

Shadows—the Three Wise Men

String puppets made by juniors

Puppets from *Hiawatha*. Back-cloth painted by children with powder paint on cotton material

Acting in the playground

Stage improvised from a clothes-horse (the play is *The Owl and the Pussy-cat*)

Spontaneous classroom acting

A shadow puppet show

Author's Preface

THIS manual began as a notebook while I was instructing teachers and students in the making of puppets. I was always asked a great many questions regarding the introduction and use of the craft in the classroom, and I hope that in this book I have provided the answers. A primary school teacher is usually responsible for most of the instruction in the classroom, so I have endeavoured to show how an active interest in puppetry can be used as an aid in the teaching of the other subjects in the curriculum.

The plays included in the book were created by children, and the manipulation is well within their capabilities. Children, if allowed to act freely, will often surprise the adult by the high standards of their work.

Puppetry can be an important activity for all ages, and the construction and manipulation of the puppets help to develop powers of initiative as well as inventive and creative faculties. The choice of plays is not subject to the usual physical limitations, and with a puppet one can be as easily a magic horse as a fairy godmother. Well-known or original stories and historical events dramatise well, and the puppeteer must use his judgement regarding the selection of material, and make practical use of research for costume design and architecture.

I should like to record my thanks to Mr. George Speaight, author of *The History of the English Puppet Theatre*, for his help with the chapter on the history of puppetry. I am also indebted to the various members of my staff who became interested in puppetry, and co-operated with me so wonderfully when I was working with children.

To conclude, the constructional information in this book, which has been collected over the past twenty years, from many and now untraceable sources, has been tempered by personal experience, and should therefore be of the greatest help to all interested in puppetry.

M.B.

PART ONE

ABOUT PUPPETRY

I: How to Introduce and Teach Puppetry in the Classroom

THERE is a tendency for some teachers to think that puppetry is only for the specialist, that the making of puppets can only be taught by the craft or art teachers, and that the play must be produced by the English specialist. This is, of course, a fallacy, especially in the primary school, for puppetry can be taught, and excellent results obtained, by any intelligent teacher provided he is interested in the subject. Most children nowadays have seen puppets on the television, but surprisingly few have actually possessed one. Bearing these facts in mind it follows that to satisfy the children there should be facilities for the making of puppets in every classroom, with the materials for making easily accessible; and also opportunities for the children to use puppets already completed. Not only does the latter stimulate a child's interest and give him a desire to create and possess one, but it also prevents him being denied the pleasure of using a puppet, simply because he is unlucky enough to have a teacher who is not interested in the subject.

Puppets are best introduced to the very young child by someone with whom he is familiar, and it should be done leisurely. I remember, one Christmas, seeing a professional puppeteer give a performance to young children, and he gave a very entertaining show. However, at the end of the entertainment, with the best of intentions, he brought a large puppet outside of his stage, and held it close to the small children in the front of the audience; and they were really frightened. Until that moment the puppet had been real to them and part of the story, but away from its character it seemed grotesque and unfamiliar.

A good way of introducing puppetry to children of any age is to take a puppet on one's own hand and tell any story suitable to that particular age group. The puppet can be made to listen to the story, or he can himself be one of the characters in the story and occasionally speak. If a teacher finds it difficult to tell a story and at the same time manipulate a puppet in front of an audience, I advise him to tell his story behind the friendly shelter of a screen, and then all his difficulties will disappear as the children concentrate and watch the puppet. In the beginning stages no teacher need worry whether his manipulation is good or bad, for I can assure him that the children will adore his efforts, think him extremely clever, and be entirely engrossed in the entertainment. Once a child's interest is aroused he becomes most enthusiastic, and it is an extremely easy task to satisfy his needs and allow him to make his own puppet. Nevertheless there are teachers who intensely desire to introduce puppetry to their children, but who doubt whether their story-telling and manipulation will sufficiently stir the interest of their pupils. For these I suggest one of the following introductions:

1. Arrange for an informal discussion about a puppet show that has been seen by the children on the television. This discussion can be with a small group or with a whole class. Alternatively a class can be divided into groups each with a child leader, and the groups can discuss separately certain aspects of the show. Later each leader can speak for his group in a combined discussion. Follow up the discussion by asking for suggestions for a story that could be made into a puppet play.

2. Ask any children in the class who possess puppets to bring them to school, and invite these children to give short group or individual shows. Follow up by asking the children if they would like to make their own puppets and use them in a play.

3. Invite a professional puppeteer to come to the school to give a show and afterwards ask the children to draw and write about it. Certain children will show definite interest, in the story, the puppets, the scenery, the stage, etc. Gather these particular children together and ask them if they would like to produce a puppet show, each trying to organise the aspect he likes best.

4. Find out where a puppet show, or an exhibition, or a puppet festival is being held, and take the children to see it. Follow up the visit with discussion, writing and drawing, and a desire to make puppets will usually come naturally and spontaneously.

5. If you are a head-teacher and wish to have puppets made in your school, but have no teachers interested, install (as I did in my school) a puppet stage for communal use in the school hall, for this never fails to cause comment and speculation, and most children eventually ask "When are we going to have a show?" I usually contrived to give a few minutes' entertainment

How to Introduce and Teach Puppetry in the Classroom 17

myself with puppets after some of the Assemblies. The entertainment took various forms—a puppet talking—a very short play usually based on a folk story, but sometimes a story pointing a moral. In a very short time it was possible to invite one or two children to help me, and gradually I was able to become a spectator, and the children were giving their own little prepared plays. For these plays the children were using puppets supplied by me, but of course the children wanted to have their own creations. I therefore asked the teachers if they could spare one or two of their children for short periods as I wished to teach them to make puppets, and I worked with these children in my own room. If I knew that a teacher was interested I asked her if she would allow me to come into her classroom, during an active period of work, to teach a group of children to make puppets. This is quite the most satisfactory method as it often attracts the teacher at the same time as the children, and many teachers upon seeing the enthusiasm of the children become enthusiastic too.

As I mentioned before, it is wise to have the materials for the making of the puppets easily available for the children in every classroom, but this does not mean that puppetry should be introduced immediately a teacher gets a new set of children. The children must first be given time to adjust themselves to their new environment and the personality of the teacher. There are always certain occupations and skills that take priority, but fortunately there does come a time when most children can work happily at various interests without the constant guidance of the teacher; and then is the time to introduce puppetry.

The class should be set to work understanding that the teacher is not available for general help, and the group of children interested in making puppets and with whom the teacher is working, should gather round a table upon which have been put all the materials for the making. It is a good idea for the teacher to sit down at the table too, and using materials begin himself to make a puppet. The children will watch for a while, but with very little encouragement will begin to make one also, sometimes imitating, and sometimes making a completely different one. First puppets are not always very well finished, but the children should be encouraged to put their maximum efforts into their work. To avoid disappointment, and to keep the interest alive, it is wise to choose a simple and quick method of making, for success with his first effort seems to make a child desire to produce a more lasting puppet requiring greater skill. A child should always be allowed to keep the first puppet he makes, and he should be allowed to play with it freely and without supervision.

The simple and quickly made puppet has another use even when children are accomplished puppeteers. Having made up a puppet play there is often a need to act it quickly before the enthusiasm is lost. Sometimes, therefore, puppets must be made quickly and used immediately. When however it is decided that a play is worth while and could be produced for a more finished performance, the puppet heads should be especially modelled to suit certain characters and strong enough to stand up to much use. The creative energy will not have been dulled, and the standard of making for the final show itself will be high because the children have not been hasty.

After children have made their first glove puppets they sometimes need guidance and help with the manipulation. Then the teacher can suggest that, either alone or with other children, they should try and make the puppet do the following:

1. Clap.
2. Bow.
3. Slap.
4. Kiss.
5. Stroke.
6. Twist.
7. Fall.
8. Rub stomach.
9. Rub eye.
10. Rub head.
11. Put hand to mouth.
12. Put hand to ear.
13. Shake hands.
14. Pick up articles.
15. Put down articles.
16. Move articles along edge of a table.
17. Walk by gliding.
18. Push with one hand.
19. Pull with two hands.
20. Nod and shake head.
21. Shake fist.
22. Hide face in hands and weep.
23. Chase one another with dodging.
24. Dance together.

II: Elementary Puppet-making

SIMPLE GLOVE PUPPET

THIS puppet can be made by very young children.

Materials. Rubber ball, potato, apple, carrot, turnip, or any similar article. Piece of cloth or small handkerchief.

Method:
1. Paint the eyes, nose and mouth, on to whatever article is used.
2. Cut a hole at the base of the head to fit the first finger.
3. Place the handkerchief over the first finger, and slip it into the hole in the head (see diagrams).
4. A modelling stand can be made by an adult by using a $\frac{3}{4}$ in. or 1 in. dowel set in a wooden base, on which to stand the head.

USEFUL PAPER PUPPET

1. Take two large sheets of kitchen paper or newspaper and fold at the centre crease. Roll these to make the body and legs. A half sheet of paper rolled makes the arms. Sheets from the *Radio Times* are suitable for a smaller puppet.
2. Cut a face from a magazine, stick it at the top of the folded roll to make the head (see diagrams). Hair can be made from tissue paper painted any colour and curled with a ruler.
3. Dress the puppet with paper skirt to form a glove. An excellent hat can be made by cutting two circles of stiff paper $3\frac{1}{2}$ in. in diameter. Cut out a small circle in the middle. Cut a circle of tissue paper $3\frac{1}{2}$ in. in diameter and push it through the hole of one of the stiff circles. This makes the crown of the hat. Stick the second circle of stiff paper on to the first to hide the join of the crown (see diagrams).

1. Puppets for young children

Elementary Puppet-making

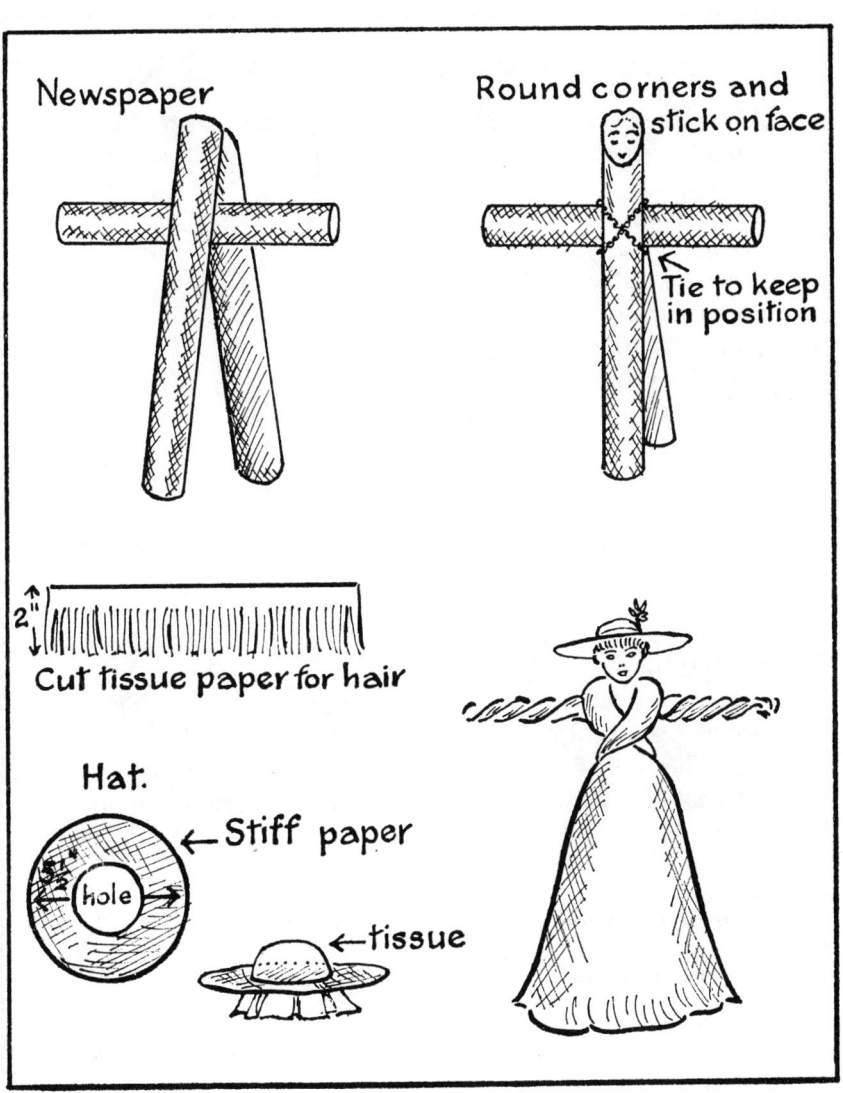

2. Simple paper puppet

GLOVE PUPPET WITH PAPIER MÂCHÉ HEAD (Paste and paper)

Materials. Back of exercise book or any stiff paper. Plasticine. Paint. Paper serviettes or tissue paper, white if possible. Paste and glue.

Method:

1. Take a piece of stiff paper about 8 in. by 6in. and twist it round the first finger; fold over the top and tie down with thread, thin string, or Sellotape (1 in Diagram 3).

2. Take some strips of soft paper about 8 in. by 22 in., crumple, twist round the top end of the finger tube (as made in 1) press to make as compact as possible. Three or four strips are usually sufficient. Tie down with thread, thin string or Sellotape (2).

3. Take a piece of Plasticine about the size of a plum, and model into a very thin plate about 3 in. by 4 in. in diameter (thin to reduce head weight). Put this plate on the side of the head and press well down (3).

4. Model a face on the Plasticine, exaggerating the features to the point of the grotesque (4).

5. Tear a paper serviette or thin paper into pieces about the size of a stamp. Using a stiff brush put a layer of paste over the whole head, then paste the pieces of paper on to the head, going well into the modelling of the eyes, nose and mouth. Put on three or four layers, and remember to cover the neck as well. If children are making these heads let each layer of paste be a different colour to check on the number of layers (5).

6. When all the layers are finished and the head is quite dry, paint and make the hair.

7. A simple glove can be made as follows: take a piece of material 6 in wide, which when folded is long enough to cover the forearm. The sides are seamed to within about an inch from the top and the child's fingers will go through the holes for arms. Cut a slit for the neck—not a hole—and stick the dress to the puppet's neck with Seccotine.

8. When making a more elaborate tunic it should be remembered that, due to the shape of the hand, one arm of the puppet will be higher than the other.

Elementary Puppet-making 23

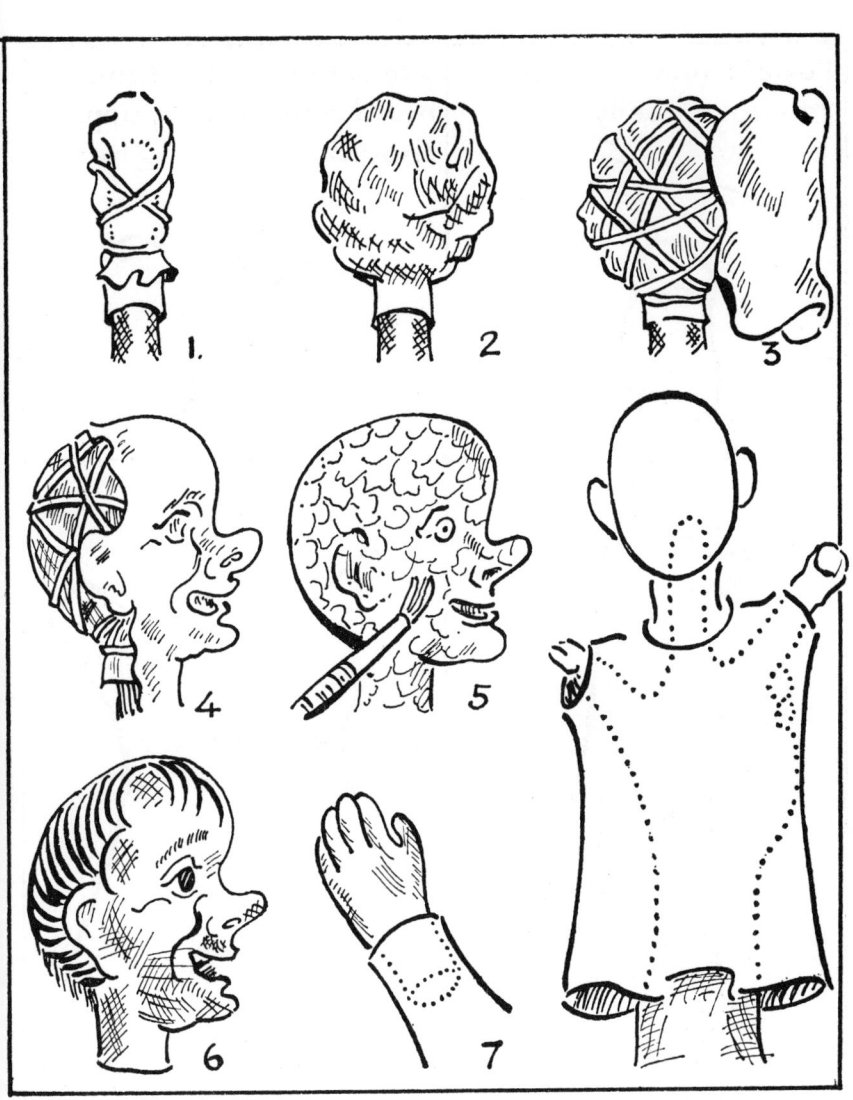

3. *A paste and paper head*

4. Some points in glove-making

GLOVE MAKING

As the methods of making heads become more skilled, so too should the making of the gloves. The very young child is content to take a square of material, put it over his hand and thrust his first finger into the head of the puppet. Children of about six years are capable of taking a piece of material about 6 in. by 18 in. and folding it in half. They can then tack the sides together, leaving open sufficient of the seams to allow them to put their finger and thumb through. Children over eight can measure their own materials more carefully and cut their own simple paper patterns. Later the glove should take a definite shape fitting individual hands, and it is wise to make a foundation glove on which to sew the costume. The foundation glove should have a wire threaded through the hem at the open end, and a ring or hook should be attached so that the puppet can be suspended upside down in the most convenient place in the stage ready for the puppeteer to slip his hand in easily.

COSTUMES

Dressing string puppets requires greater skill and the costumes should be built directly on to the puppet, first the sleeves, then the bodice and last the skirt, and all sewn securely together. It is not necessary to produce the costumes in great detail, but characteristics of a person or period should be accentuated. Before actually cutting the materials for the costumes, it is advisable to test out the colours under the stage lighting, for the colours seem to change under strong artificial light. A pale pink may look dirty white, a small print become indeterminate, or a purple seem dusty black.

ANIMAL PUPPETS FROM WASTE MATERIAL

Animal puppets are funnier if not too realistic, but they should be as flexible as possible. They can be made of any material—cloth, fur, leather, plush, etc.

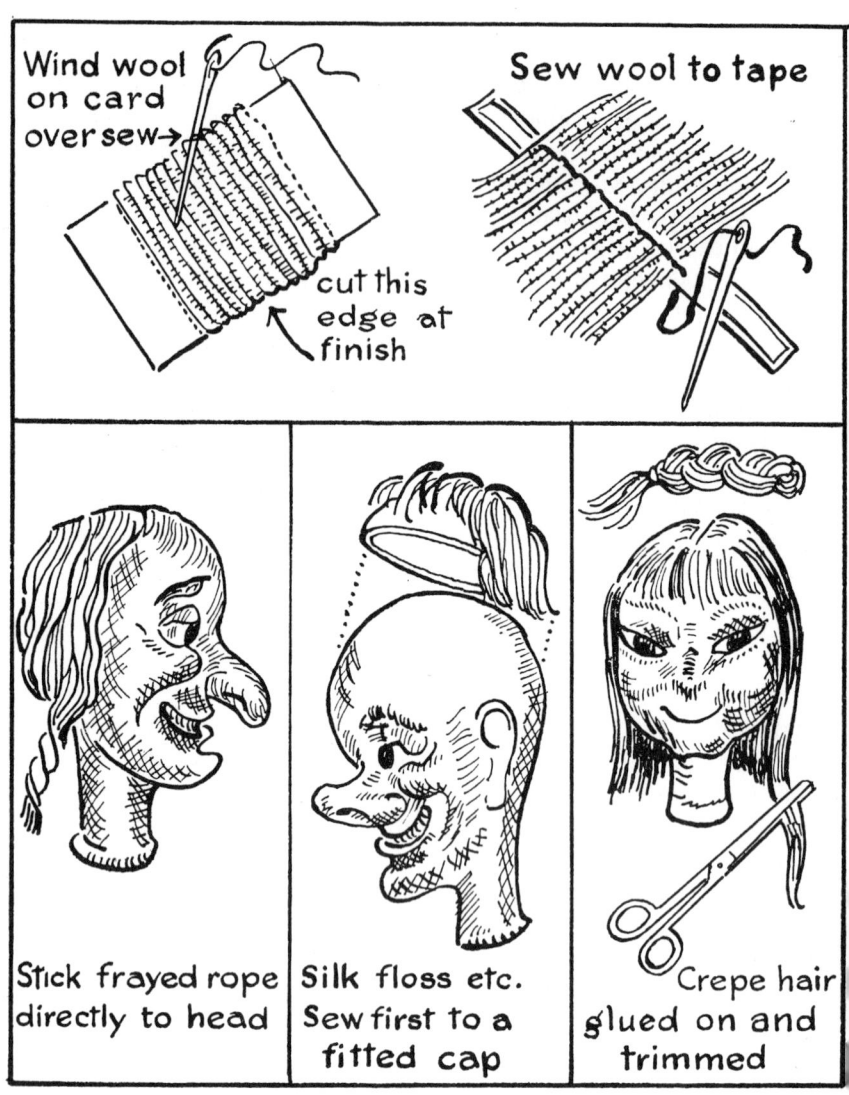

5. *The making of wigs*

Elementary Puppet-making

A dragon often needs movable jaws, and leather is useful to obtain this effect.

Snakes and reptiles can be made from old stockings. Put the hand into the toe of the stocking, stretch the fingers and draw them together to a point to make a snaky head. Use old beads or buttons for the eyes and decorate the stocking with sequins or gilt paint.

Cotton reels joined together make a centipede, especially if springs are fixed for feet. If small balls can be obtained they are more satisfactory than cotton reels.

When making animal string puppets, an inside construction of wood or cardboard will help to hold out the body, with the contour and shape stuffed with cotton. Sometimes sticks inside cloth legs will stiffen them. Always weight the feet well.

Legs on string puppets may be attached by wire run through the body or else by chamois or leather hinges. The legs must swing easily.

Fascinating odd animals can be made by using small discarded boxes for bodies and heads. Corks stuck to the faces make good noses and tails can be made of unravelled rope yarn.

ADDITIONAL HEADS

BUCKRAM HEAD. Model head in Plasticine and cut it into two pieces to make a back and a front of a head. Take a piece of thin buckram, larger than the front of the head, soften in hot water and, using the buckram on the bias, lay it over the Plasticine model. Force it well down ino the eyes, mouth, sides of nose, etc. Take some dressmaker's pins and stick these through the buckram into the Plasticine around the base of the nose, the eyes, and the mouth. It may be necessary to cut the buckram to make it fit, and then overlap it. The pins will hold it down and keep it in shape until it dries stiff. When it is dry shellac it thoroughly. When the shellac is dry remove the pins, cut out the Plasticine, and then crumple up some newspaper and glue and place this inside the head. Join the front and back of the head together with adhesive tape, or cloth dipped in glue. Paint as desired.

PLASTER OR "POLYFILLA" HEAD. Cut up 1 in. cotton bandage into 1 in lengths. Model a head with Plasticine and cut it into

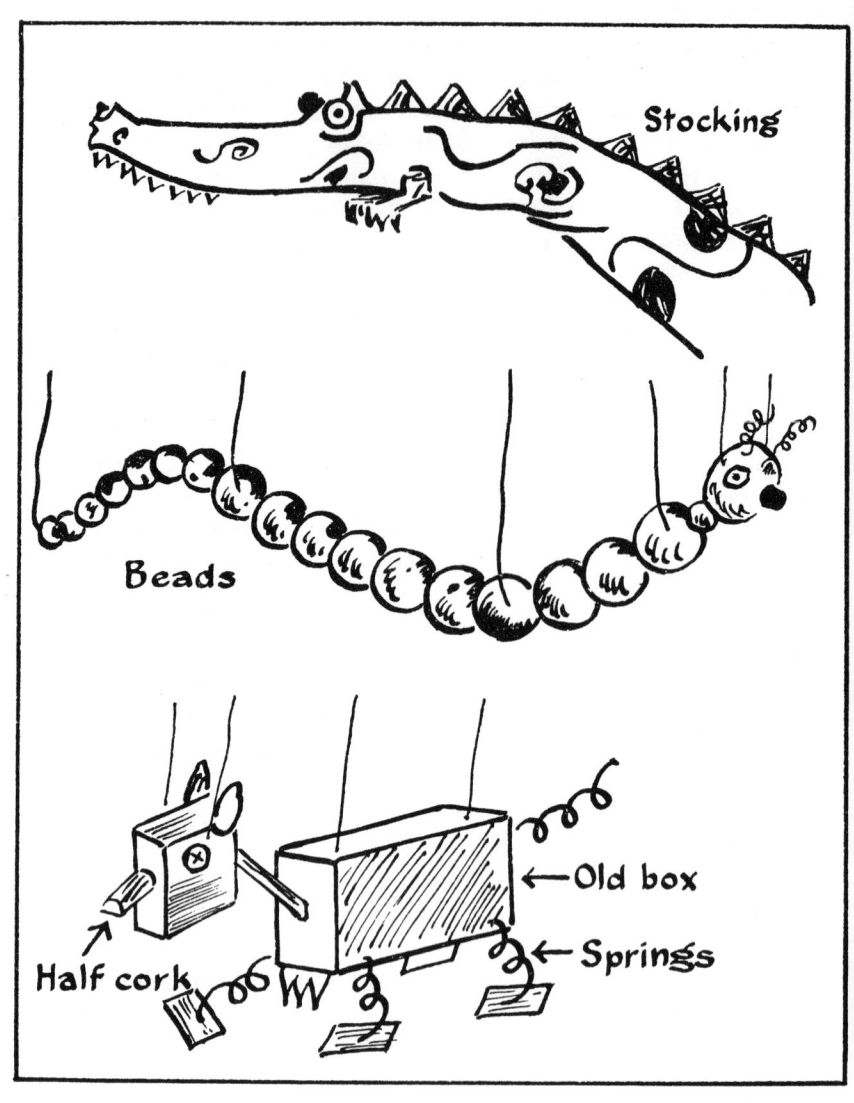

6. *Puppets from waste material*

Elementary Puppet-making

two pieces to make a back and a front of a head. Cover the face and the back of the head with Vaseline or wet paper to prevent the plaster sticking to the Plasticine. Dip the pieces of cotton bandage into the Polyfilla and lay them all over the face and the back of the head, making sure that they overlap. The cotton will stretch and bend into almost any shape or corner. Put on about three layers, leave to dry, and then remove the Plasticine from the inside. Join the two halves together with bandage and paint the whole head.

CURTAINS AND STAGES

For glove puppets a collapsible and portable booth is better than a solid one, and the proscenium opening varies according to the size of the puppets. From 2 ft. to 5 ft. long and from 15 in. to 25 in. high is a satisfactory opening. The manipulator can sit or stand, and the best lighting is produced by a small set of strip lights just below and above the proscenium opening.

A marionette stage can also be portable. The proscenium opening will vary according to the size of the string puppets, but it is usually from $2\frac{1}{2}$ ft. to $3\frac{1}{2}$ ft. high, and from 5 ft. to 7 ft. long. An opening 3 ft. by 6 ft. is a good size to use with puppets of 18 in. to 22 in. The bridge rails should be waist high and it is a good idea to place a board in front of the bridge to keep the puppeteers from kicking the settings. The stage floor should be $2\frac{1}{2}$ ft. to 4 ft. deep, depending upon the size of the proscenium opening.

BACK-CLOTHS

Back-cloths made of material are in some ways better than solid "backs", for they can be folded and packed with little trouble. Cut unbleached calico or cotton material to the size required, lay it on the floor and draw details with a piece of black waxed crayon. The waxed crayon will keep the colours from spreading. Colour inks are good for painting, but powder paint can be used successfully. Jam-jars make excellent containers as enough colour can then be mixed before starting. Fill each jar almost full of water, and put in ink until the colour is the required shade or tint. Take a tube of white water colour paint and squeeze

7. *Simple masking and curtains*

Elementary Puppet-making

in about half a teaspoonful to a quart of liquid. This is to make the tint slightly opaque. Rub a piece of soap with a wet brush and stir enough soap into the mixture with the brush to bring bubbles to the surface. This acts as a binder and will make the colours go on evenly, smoothly and flat, without globules of moisture. It is wise to experiment on a small piece of cloth first. Put newspapers under the material to absorb any colour which might go through, and do not paint over the wax lines. Tack the back-cloth on to a wood strip at the top (and the bottom if desired) and fix to the rail at the back of the stage. Slits can be cut up the cloth from the bottom, and these can be used for entrances and exits. This is especially useful when working with young children.

USEFUL HINTS

When painting heads, turn on the stage lights and put the puppets on the stage, walk about twenty feet away and see if all the features carry.

A pure white skin looks ghastly, but can be used for a ghost or a clown.

Unity should be preserved in puppets, so do not use twenty-four-inch puppets with twelve-inch ones. Also try not to use wooden puppets with cloth ones unless striving for some definite effect.

When learning to manipulate a puppet sometimes work in front of a mirror in order to watch the results.

To make a coat of mail, take an old turkish towel, cut to a mail pattern, and then paint the surface with aluminium paint. Rub in well with the fingers and leave to dry. When dry brush the surface to remove superfluous silver and raise nap.

Stained glass windows can be made by drawing on tracing paper and then painting with coloured dyes. Fasten to the window opening and place a light behind it.

When dressing a string puppet it is best to sew or tack the costume on to the puppet piece by piece. For instance, put on the sleeves first, then the bodice and then the skirt.

Necks of string puppets can be disguised with chamois leather or flesh-coloured silk. Always exaggerate the size of head, hands and feet.

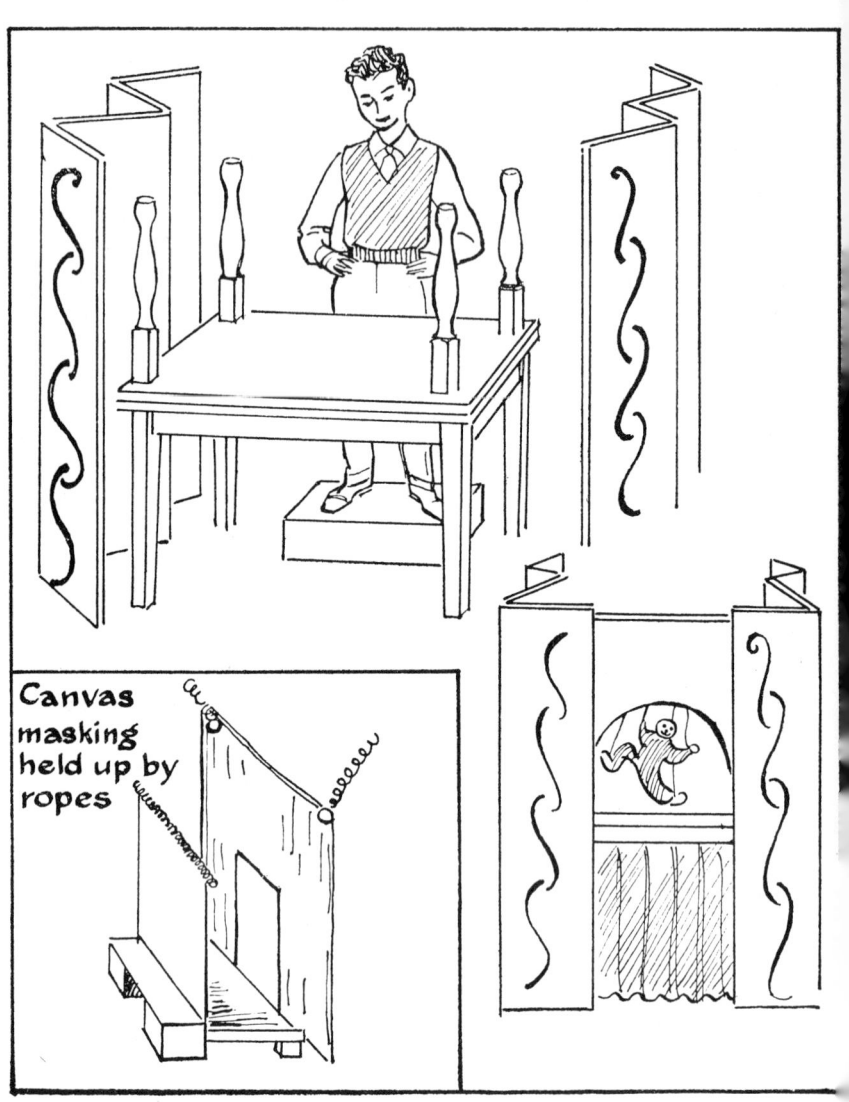

8. *An improvised stage*

To prevent any piece of property in a string puppet play from toppling, attach a large piece of cardboard or thin three-ply wood to the bottom with nails, glue or screws. Cover this with the same material as is on the floor (velvet is excellent).

WIGS

When making hair to put on the puppet, use the toe or heel of a stocking for a foundation. and on to this sew yarn, lamb's wool, or strips of cloth. These may be dyed any colour before they are put on to the foundation, and then stuck on to the head after the face has been painted. Fur makes good hair and does not need a stocking foundation. Steel wool is excellent for Negroid hair, while a copper scourer can be used for golden curls.

HANDS

It is a good idea when making hands to form a small ring of cardboard to fit the tops of the finger and thumb which are to be used for the puppet's arms. The cloth hand can be stuck to this and the whole attached to the glove.

Hands can be made quite easily with wire, copper wire being the best; hat wire is quite successful. First form the wire into the shape of the hand, and then build up the fingers and palm with Plasticine, and finally cover the whole with papier mâché and paint.

Wooden hands are good, but never, unless extremely skilful at carving, cut the fingers separately, because they will only get broken. A box from any grocer makes excellent wood for carving.

9. *Types of wig*

Elementary Puppet-making

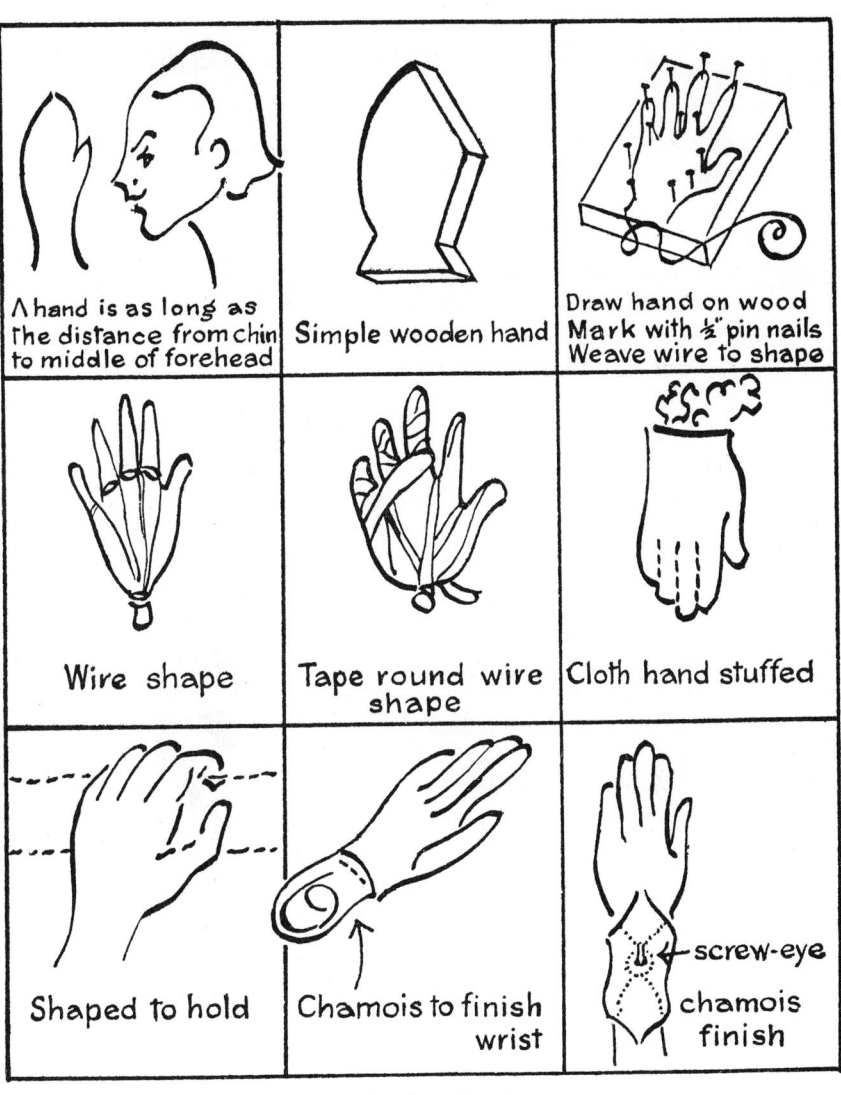

10. *Making hands*

III: How to Make Papier Mâché

PAPIER MÂCHÉ WHEN HARD CAN BE SANDPAPERED, SAWN OR CUT WITH A KNIFE.

Method:
1. Use the softer, poorer quality newspaper.
2. Tear the newspaper into small pieces. Place in a bucket or similar receptacle.
3. Pour on a liberal quantity of water. Hot water is better than cold.
4. The paper must be made to disintegrate. Moulding and rubbing with the hands is the best way. (Children seem to be prepared to play with the "mash" for long periods.) If it is impossible to obtain this "hand-work", then boiling the mixture helps, or soaking for three or four days. The pulp is ready when there are no pieces of paper recognisable and the whole is an even colour and texture.
5. Get rid of the surplus water. The best way to do this is to put the pulp into a cloth and wring it out. If desired the pulp can now be dried out and kept indefinitely, re-soaking before adding paste.
6. Having got rid of the surplus water shake powder paste, a little at a time, on to the pulp. Mould together as though making a dough, only adding extra water to make the mixture malleable and cohesive. It should not be so dry that the resulting mixture breaks when pressed, nor so wet that it exudes paste. It is difficult to estimate the exact quantities . . . it is something that is learnt with experience, but use roughly about 1 oz. of dry paste (3 level tablespoons) to 1 lb. of wrung pulp. Eight single sheets of newspaper make about 1 lb. pulp.

IV: How to Make and Manipulate String Puppets

FIRST STRING PUPPET

Materials. Ten pieces of paper 2 in. by 24 in. One piece of paper 2½ in. by 24 in. Two cardboard feet and two cardboard hands (see diagrams). Linen tape or adhesive tape. String.

Method:
 1. Make ten tubes by rolling the ten pieces of paper, each tube being 2 in. long. Make one tube 2½ in. long. Take the wide tube and two of the smaller ones and bind them together with the tape to make the body (see diagram).
 2. Tie a piece of string to one cardboard foot and then proceed to string as indicated by the arrow in diagram 2. Use two tubes for each leg and two for each arm. The tubes can be improved by painting them with white paint.
 3. Make a papier mâché head and continue the string through the centre of the head.
 4. Attach the strings from the legs to a piece of wood about 6 in. by ¾ in. and the head and hand strings to another piece of wood of the same size to make simple wooden controls.

WOODEN STRING PUPPET

Materials. Three blocks of wood measuring 2 in. by 1¼ in. by ¼ in. Four ½ in. dowels 2 in. long; cut down the centre of each one to make eight half dowels. Two ½ in. dowels 1 in. long, one cut down the centre. Strips of leather about ½ in. wide.

Method:
 1. Make the legs by sticking four of the half dowels on to two pieces of leather, leaving a small space of about ⅛ in. between the pieces of wood to make a knee joint. Sufficient lengths of leather should be left at the ends to enable the legs to be stuck to one of

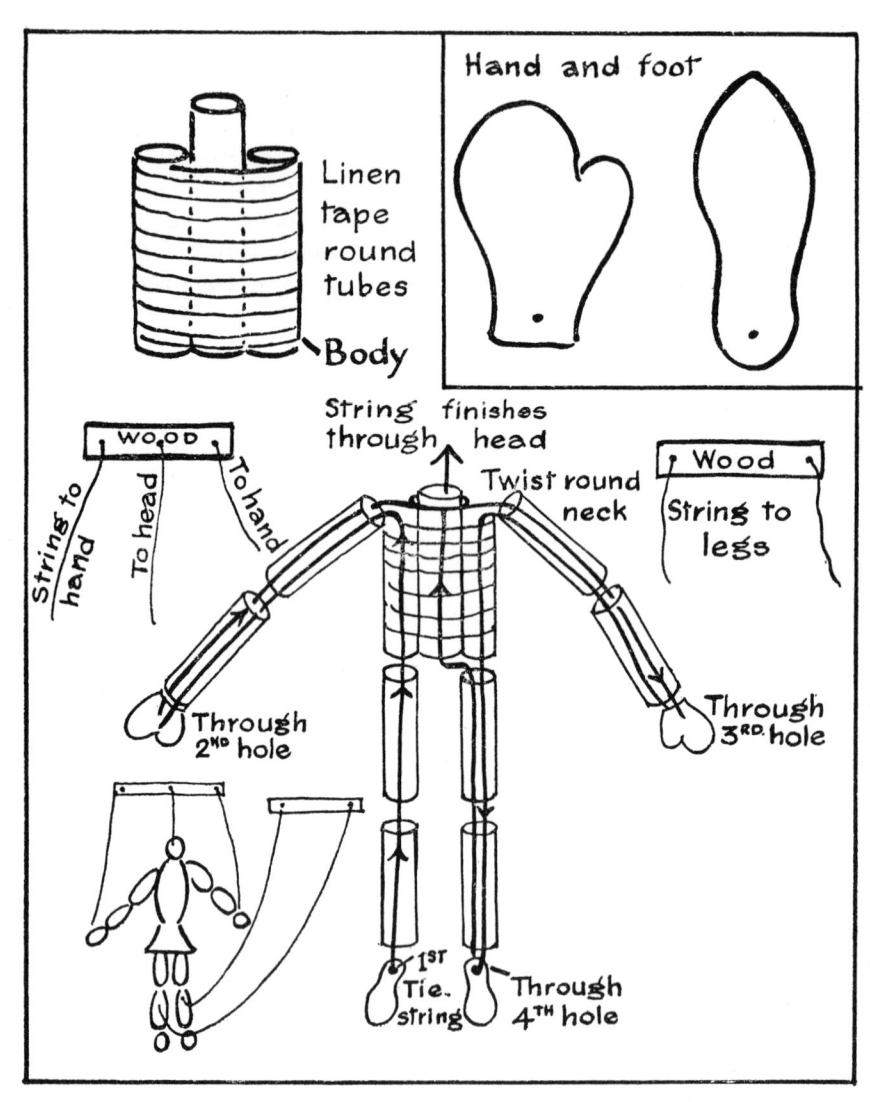

11. Simple string puppet

How to Make and Manipulate String Puppets

the blocks of wood (see diagram). The other block of wood should then be stuck to the first to enclose the leather ends. These two blocks form the hips of the puppet.

2. The arms are made similarly to the legs, except that both arms are stuck to the same piece of leather (see diagram). Leave about $2\frac{1}{2}$ in. in the centre between the arm dowels and tack this piece of leather to the top of the third block of wood (see diagram). This block forms the chest of the puppet.

3. Drill a hole in a small round dowel, and use this for a neck. Thread a piece of string through the hole. Make a hole in the block of wood supporting the arms, about $\frac{1}{4}$ in. from the top edge, and thread the string through. Tie the string.

4. Drill a hole through the two blocks stuck together, and drill another hole about $\frac{1}{4}$ in. from the bottom of the chest block. Fasten the chest block and the hips block together with a loose string. The string must be loose in order to make a body for the puppet and to give it freedom (see diagram).

5. Stick the two small half dowels to the leg leathers to make the feet, leaving space for the ankle joint.

6. The head can be made with papier mâché. The hands and the feet can be modelled in many ways as described elsewhere in this book.

FEET FOR STRING PUPPETS

Feet can either be modelled directly on to the puppet with no joint or made with a joint at the ankle. It is usually necessary to weight the feet and there are various ways of doing this.

1. Cut from a piece of sheet lead $\frac{1}{16}$ in. thick, a piece large enough to fit the bottom of the foot. Glue this to the bottom of the foot.

2. A hole can be drilled in the bottom of the foot and filled with lead, then plastic wood can be put all over the surface.

3. With cloth puppets anything heavy can be used inside the cloth foot to weight it.

LEGS FOR STRING PUPPETS

Legs are usually made of dowelling. For 18 in. clothed puppets, $\frac{1}{2}$ in. dowels are large enough, but for 22 in. and 24 in. puppets,

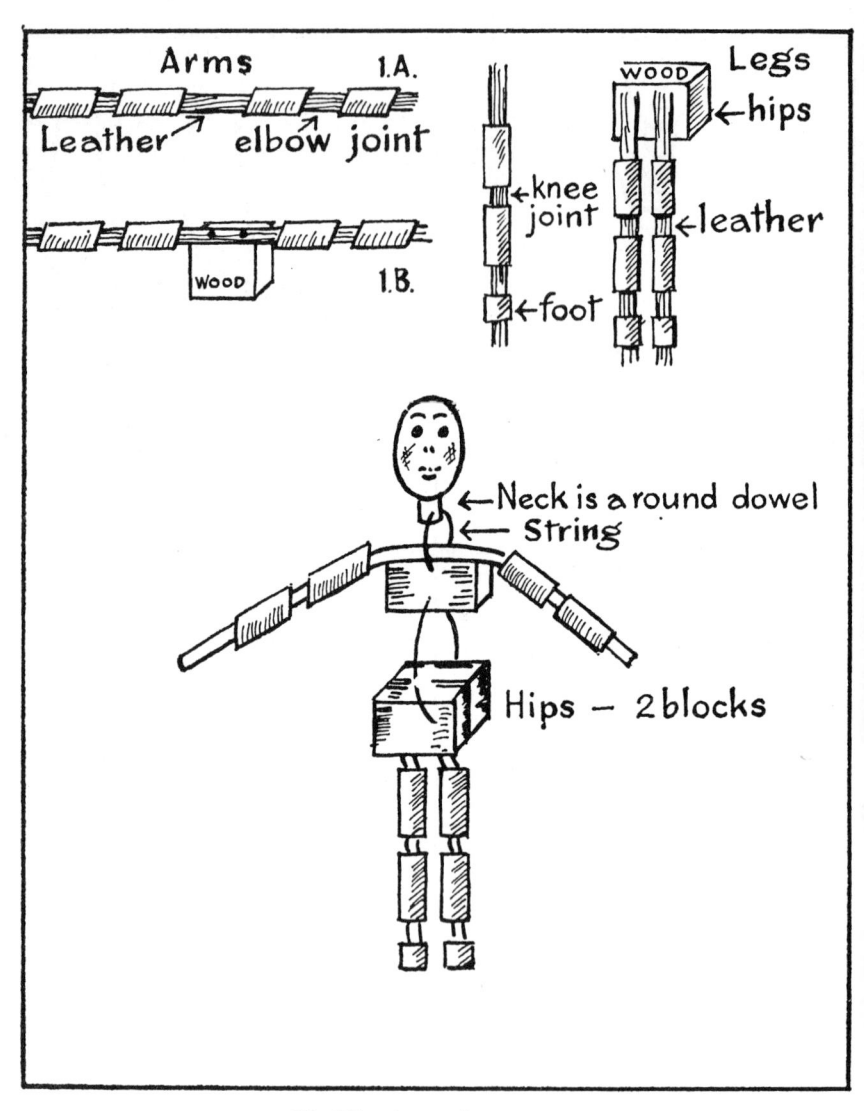

12. *Wooden string puppet*

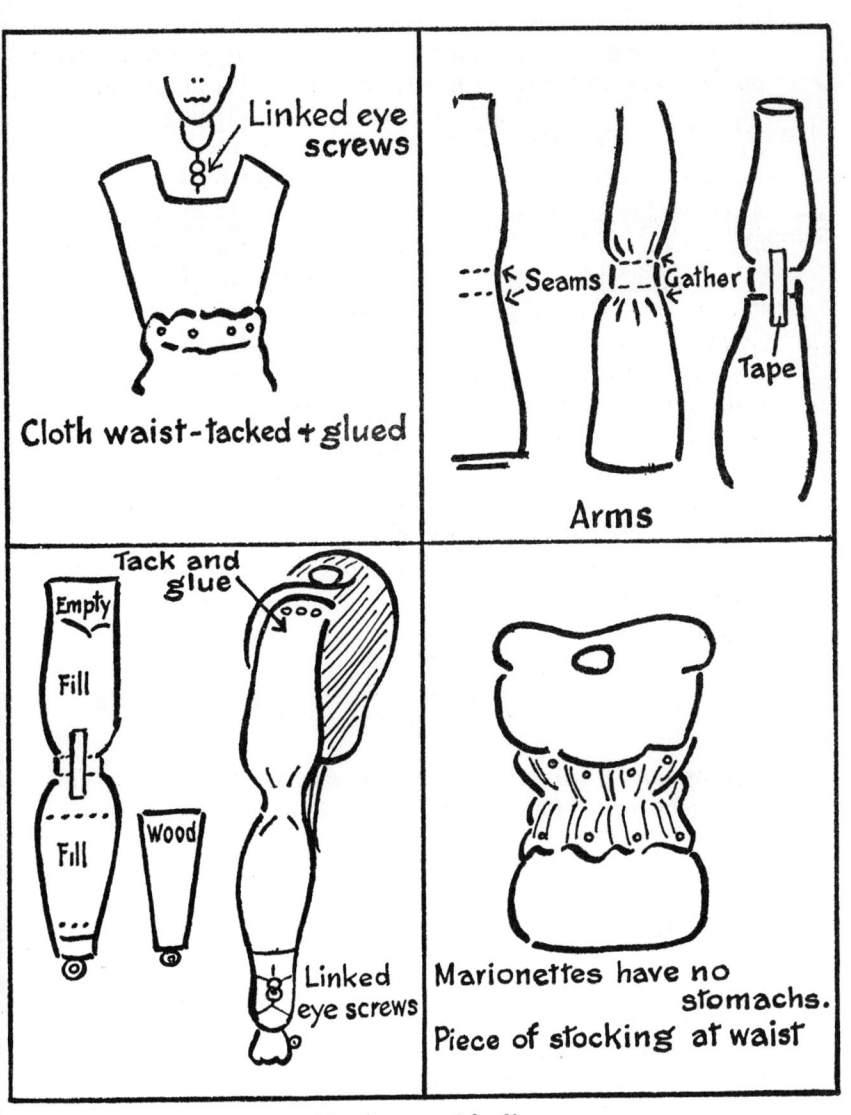

13. Arms and bodies

it is wiser to use ¾ in. dowelling. The shape of the leg can be modelled with Plasticine, papier mâché, or plastic wood, and then painted.

For the knee joint take the dowelling and cut where the knee joint is going to be, making sure that the cut is square and not running off at some unknown angle. Cut a half round piece out behind the knee, then cut slots for a piece of tin, again making sure that these do not run at an angle. Notice that the lower part of the leg pivots on the upper part. When the piece of tin is flat and the edges rounded and the right length, place the tin in the slot of the lower part of the leg; then drill two holes in the leg and the tin. Fasten the tin to the leg with copper wire through the holes. Now take the upper part of the leg, hold it very tightly in an upright position against the lower part of the leg, and again drill through the leg and the tin for the point on which the lower leg will pivot. When this is done put a piece of copper wire or nail through (see diagrams). The joint should move similarly to a human knee. If the leg bends forward, which it should not, build up the front edge of the upper and lower part of the leg with a little plastic wood. This will stop them passing each other and make the leg work correctly. Other joints are shown in the diagrams.

ARMS

Arms can be made with dowelling similarly to the legs. They can also be made of material and stuck to the body (see diagrams).

CONTROLS AND MANIPULATION

Materials. One piece of wood 10 in. by 1 in. by ¼ in. One piece of wood 7 in. by 1 in. by ¼ in. One piece of wood 9 in. by 1 in. by ¼ in. Three small screw eyes. One inch of ¼ in. dowelling for the hanging of the foot bar. Glue and tacks.

Method:
Make as in diagrams.
Be sure to dovetail the cut for the joining of the cross pieces. The slit at the end must be small enough to hold the string firmly

How to Make and Manipulate String Puppets 43

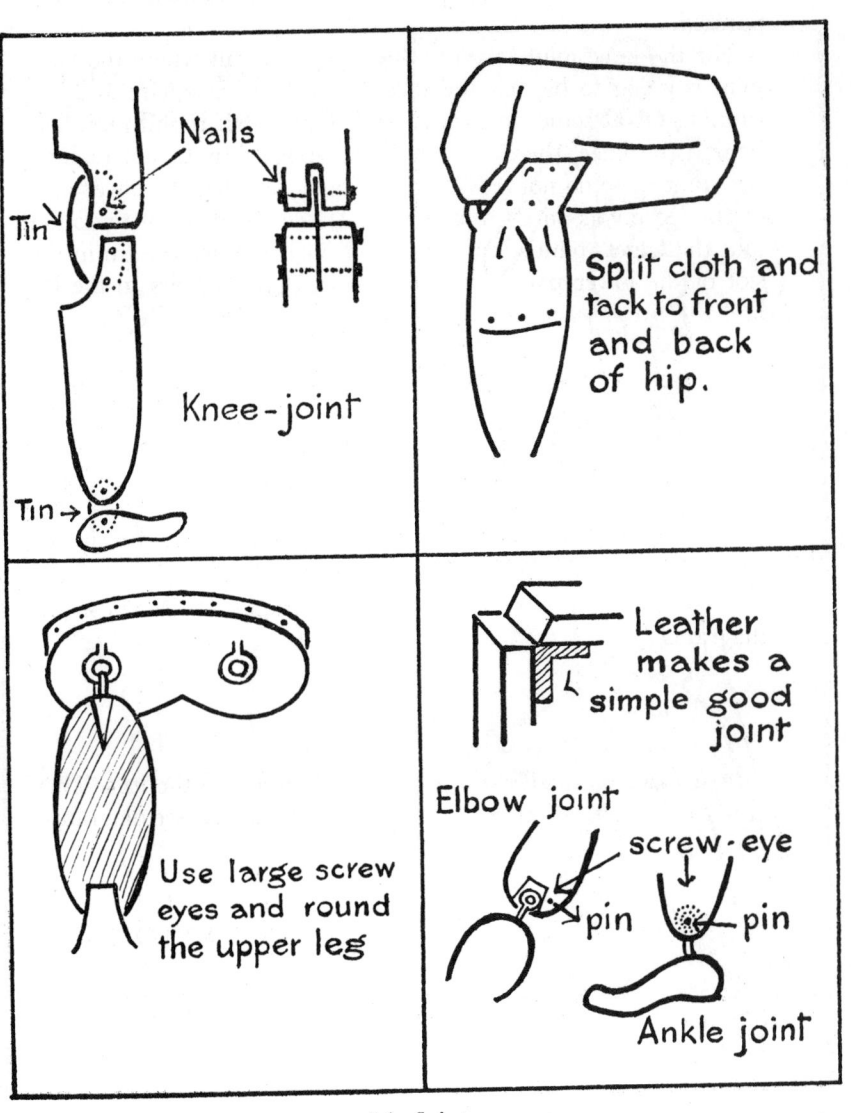

Nails

Tin

Knee-joint

Tin

Split cloth and tack to front and back of hip.

Use large screw eyes and round the upper leg

Leather makes a simple good joint

Elbow joint — screw-eye — pin

Ankle joint — pin

14. Joints

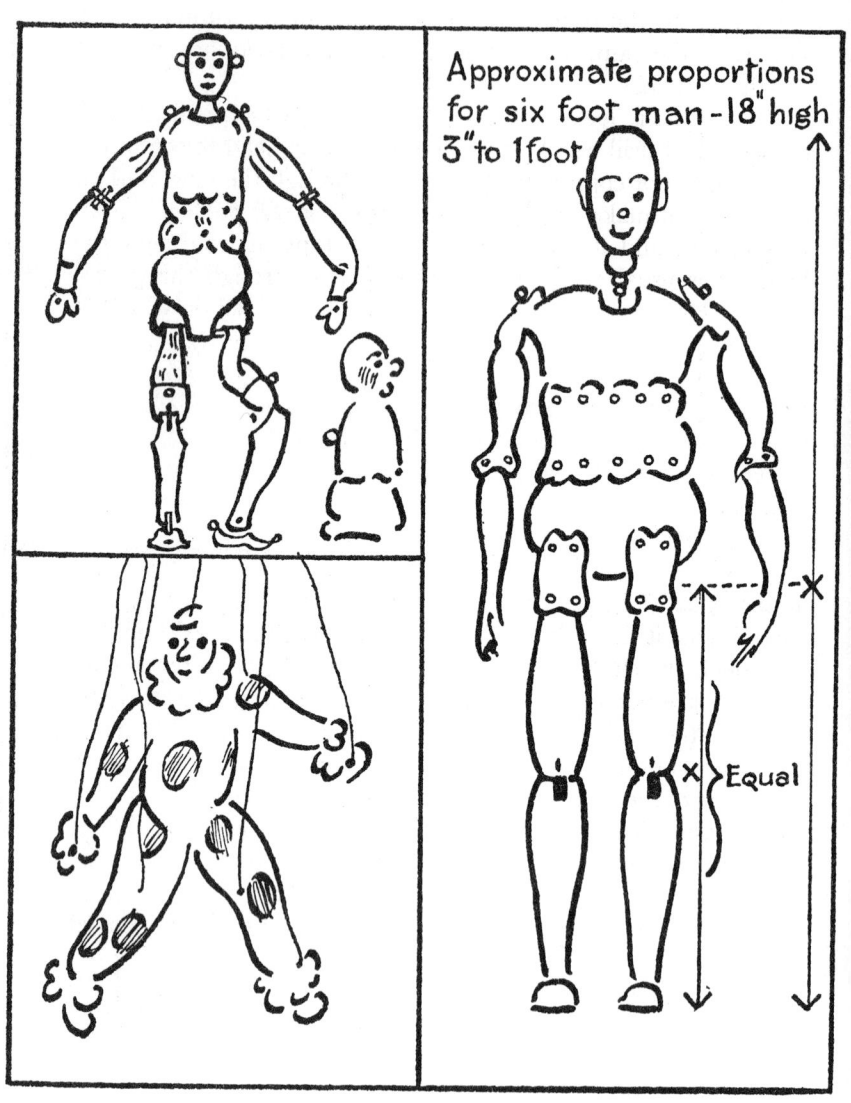

15. *Proportions for string puppet*

before it is wrapped round the notches. The screw eye beneath the control is used for the running shoulder strings. The two small screw eyes on the front of the control are for the running hand strings. If the puppet is made of wood, use tacks on which to attach the strings.

For the head, locate the point of balance, which is usually at the ears, and drill a hole from one side of the head to the other. Take a piece of copper wire and run it through the hole, and on each end of it make a small twisted loop. This will prevent it from pulling out, and it can be used on any type of head. For the hands it is usually possible to make a hole through the palms. For shoulders, knees, back strings, tacks can be used on which to attach the string.

STRINGING THE PUPPETS. The first strings to be attached are the shoulder strings, and these must always be kept taut, for if they become slack the head movements will be stiff. Next string the head strings with the same tension as the shoulder strings. The head strings must always be in front of the shoulder strings. Next comes the back string. Tie one end of the string to the screw eye at the back of the puppet. Carry it up to the back end of the control, pass it through the slit, wrap it around the wood and pass it through the slit again to ensure that it will not slip out. Leave the back string long enough to ensure that when the puppet bows its head the whole body does not bend at the waist. The hand strings are continuous running strings. The hand should be relaxed at the side of the puppet.

The last strings to be placed are the leg or foot strings. These strings should be long enough to allow for the foot bar to be placed over the small 1 in. dowel on the front of the control, so as to allow the puppet to be always in an upright and relaxed position.

For stringing use black carpet linen thread; silk fishing line is good, but this is expensive. Black has been found the best colour for strings and the direct light should be kept from them as much as possible. A plain black curtain, preferably velvet, is best for a permanent back-drop, as this makes the strings less conspicuous.

16. *String puppet stage*

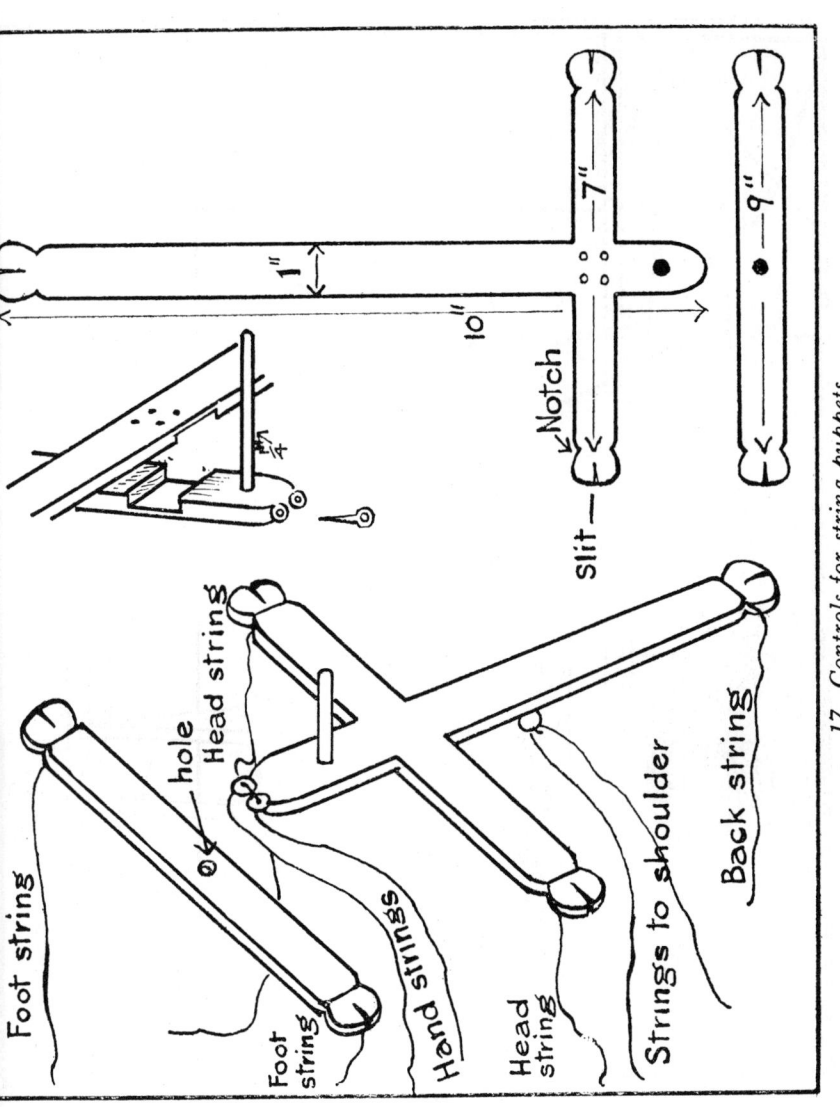

17. Controls for string puppets

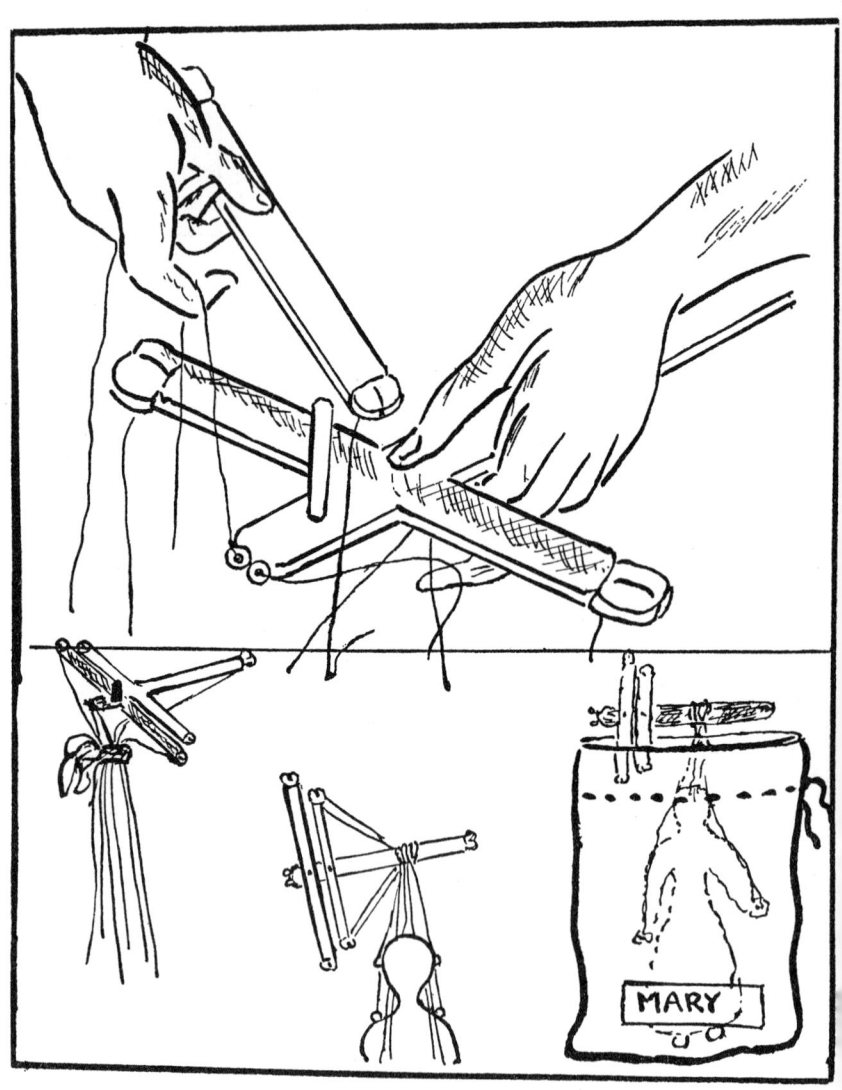

18. Manipulation

V: Shadow Puppetry

Young and old are interested in shadows, and shadows that become puppets have a great appeal. Yet it is a form of puppetry that is often neglected, although once an interest is aroused it is seldom lost. Probably only a few children in a class will want to experiment with shadows, and it will be necessary to provide these children with some form of screen on which they can practise. A very simple screen can be made from an old picture frame with tracing paper, cotton or nylon stretched across it and tacked to the back. In the beginning it is only necessary to place the frame against the light when the children will make shadows with their hands. Later they will experiment by holding up various objects close to the screen in order to see the shadows that are cast. Very soon after this experiment the children begin to cut out figures in cardboard and hold them near the screen. When cardboard figures are used it soon becomes obvious that they cannot be held in the fingers as these cast unwanted shadows, and the children will try to find suitable methods of controlling the figures. A teacher should be prepared for this contingency and have a box containing wire, wooden dowelling, matchboxes, Sellotape, paper clips, etc., for experimental purposes. There are various and obvious ways of fixing a rod to a shadow puppet, but most are good provided they are efficient and within the scope of the makers. As the children make more operative puppets they will want better lighting, and an ordinary electric light bulb hanging just above the top of the screen, and about three feet behind it, is excellent. For a more permanent stage the picture frame screen can be fixed to metal angle brackets so that it can stand on a flat surface.

The puppets are flat, and if movement is required the limbs can be cut separately and jointed. The joints can be fastened with rivet type paper clips, the round brass head of the clip to the screen, or fine wire can be twisted into flat spirals back and front of the joints; or string can be used with knots back and front. More advanced figures can be shaped in wire and covered with material.

The scenery is usually cut from cardboard and can be placed in front or back of the screen, whichever is most convenient. Adults have secured successful scenic efforts by projecting coloured transparencies of scenes on to a plain back-cloth. At one Art College I saw a very good show where the students used the shadows from their own hands under various coloured lights, with a back-cloth on which were projected transparencies made by the students showing a conglomeration of different colours and shapes. Colours on figures and scenes can be obtained by cutting them in lampshade vellum and staining the vellum, or by cutting holes and slashes in the cardboard figures and sticking coloured cellophane over the spaces.

Nursery rhymes and fairy stories are excellent material for shadow plays, and sometimes it is possible to use both glove and shadow puppets in one production. I produced a Nativity Play and fixed the shadow screen across the glove stage about eighteen inches from the front. Across this screen the Wise Men on their camels were seen travelling to Bethlehem and the effect was most intriguing, making a complete change from the gloves without spoiling the continuity. Another time one of my teachers produced a play from the poem *The Pied Piper of Hamelin*, and she asked me to help her with the problem of showing masses of children and rats following the piper. I fixed up a similar screen to the one mentioned above, and across this screen the shadow children and shadow rats passed in great numbers. The Piper remained a glove puppet the whole time and stayed in front of the shadow screen.

Sometimes shadow puppetry can be linked to centres of interest. For example a class has an interest round ships, and one of the activities connected with it is a collection of pictures of boats. A group of children can take some of the pictures and copy the boats on to drawing paper, and these copies can be pasted on to black cardboard and cut out. The children then fix control rods to these cut-outs so that, in effect, they become shadow puppets. These ships are made to cross a shadow screen and the children watching recognise and name each one as it appears. Scenery depicting dock buildings can be added, and this often necessitates much investigation and reading of reference books, so that with a little imagination and initiative many scenes can be planned. I feel certain that shadow puppetry would be used more often in schools if its possibilities were appreciated.

19. Simple shadow screen

HOW TO MAKE SHADOW PUPPETS

Materials. Thin cardboard. Drawing paper. Black cardboard or lampshade vellum. Wire for rods. Brass paper clips (rivet type) or carpet thread. Scissors.

Method:
 1. Draw the figures required on to the drawing paper, being careful to draw them in proportion to the size of the screen.
 2. Divide these drawings into movable sections but do not cut them.
 3. Trace each segment separately on to the cardboard or vellum, and then cut them out.
 4. Pierce with a needle at the points where the figures are to be jointed and join them with a clip or thread.
 5. Attach the wire rods on the figures at points where the puppets can be manipulated easily.

HINTS ON MAKING SHADOW PUPPETS

The ribs of an umbrella frame can be used as rods on shadow puppets, but they are a little thick.

A wire paper clip can be adapted to make a hook at the top of a wooden rod, and this can be inserted into a slot fixed to the puppet.

On "humans" it is wise to attach the rods to the front of the neck, so that the figure is balanced from that point.

Miraculous disappearance or appearance is achieved by drawing the shadow puppets sharply away from or towards the screen.

Scenery can be slipped between the frame of the screen and the material of the screen, or it can be nailed to the top of the screen if it is needed high up.

Coloured plastics can be used to make shadow figures.

Nail polish can be used for painting on translucent (acetate transparent) sheets.

A cotton sheet stretched across an open door will make a temporary screen.

Bamboo makes good handles

20. *Chinese type of figure*

21. Shadows

VI: Puppets for Different Age Groups

It is surprising how often only one method of making a puppet is used in a school. Surprising, because there are so many methods and materials to use that will interest the creative child, and because, as he becomes more skilled, he needs to be introduced to more difficult methods that must be a challenge to his increased abilities if his interest is to be kept. Of course, a return to a familiar and easy method of making can be fun, but in these circumstances the teacher should appreciate that a higher standard of finish should be achieved with more experience. Not only should the children be taught to use different techniques, but they should also be encouraged to invent new ways of making according to their skills and abilities. One child may wish to repeat a method of making until he is completely satisfied with the results; but another may decide that he dislikes certain materials and wishes to use different ones. The satisfaction of creating is always very great, and success usually stimulates the maker to greater efforts.

To help children to be inventive it is a good idea to keep in the classroom, for free use, a box containing all sorts of materials, as these are invaluable when gloves have to be decorated or a head needs to be original. The teacher should try to keep this box well supplied with waste materials, for as the children become more inventive they will use more and more bits and pieces. A monitor can be elected whose job it is to report to the teacher when certain stocks get low. I found that children like to have in the box such things as pieces of leather, buttons, beads, lace, fur, small sticks, cardboard, tubes, coloured paper, pieces of felt, sponge, fleece, small feathers—in fact, almost anything. Left alone to create the children seem to have an infallible sense of what is right, and the most strange colours and materials are used with delightful results. I have seen the following successfully used:

> A short piece of fringe for the mane of a horse, and a Vim box for the body.
> Small pieces of lace for aprons, bonnets, a clown's ruff, a queen's crown, and a courtier's cuffs.

A head covered with a piece of towelling to make a rabbit with pink felt inside his ears.

Brass paper clips pierced into a strip of leather for a cowboy's belt.

Beads, buttons and felt for eyes.

The following is a broad outline of types of heads for children to make at various ages and each within the making capacity of the child. Obviously the abilities and interests cannot be confined to certain ages so this can only be a suggested list.

4-6 years.   Potatoes, carrots, apples, and any suitable vegetables or fruit.
Tins, cardboard boxes, painted paper, paper bags, cardboard tubes, tennis and table tennis balls, old socks.
Solid papier mâché. (See instructions earlier for making.)

7-8 years.   Solid papier mâché; this is especially good for animals.
Simple string puppets of waste materials, e.g. newspaper animals or cardboard boxes.
Paper doll puppets. See diagrams (page 21).
Free creative work with waste materials.
Shadows.

8-11 years.   Solid papier mâché.
Hollow heads covered with papier mâché.
String puppets with "bodies" of rolled paper tubes.
Free creative work.
Shadows.

11-15 years.   Hollow heads with various materials for covering.
Solid papier mâché heads. The papier mâché should be of a fine mix and the finished head should be sandpapered to a smooth surface.
Carved wooden heads.
String puppets with wooden block "bodies" and with jointed arms and legs.

Puppets for Different Age Groups

                Free creative work.
                Masks.
                Shadows.

15 and over.   As above.
                Rod puppets.
                Marionettes with full stringing.
                Glove and string heads with character impersonations.
                Heads with mobile jaws, etc.
                Trick glove and string puppets.
                Shadows.

VII: Class Production, and Stories Suitable for Plays

In an endeavour to secure a perfect production (if there is such a thing?) a producer may defeat his aim by over-rehearsing a puppet play, and then it will lose its spontaneity and fun, because the players become bored with much repetition; for this reason, if the manipulation or the speech is bad it is better to allow the players to practise these apart from the play. To me it is comparable to trying to teach someone to spell when he is struggling to write an imaginative story. How can anyone be free to let his thoughts flow if he is worrying about mechanical skills which should be practised separately? Children are usually so keen to use their puppets and take a part in a play that tactful help will in most cases make them improve their speech. Audibility depends not so much on volume of sound as on good articulation and voice production. Sometimes a producer wanting good speech will allow one player to speak and one to manipulate, but I do not favour this arrangement, for it robs the puppeteer of the pleasure of having complete control of his puppet. Having two people control one puppet can have strange effects, and it is not unknown to find that the speech and the movement do not synchronise! In senior schools where more than one teacher may be responsible for a production it is sometimes desirable for the teacher of English to be completely responsible for the spoken words, and if the school time-table makes combined practices impossible, the children can make a tape recording of the play which can be used by the manipulators and the producer.

Puppet plays written by children are seldom literary, but are often better for use than plays written for children by adults. When a speech is long it should be broken up by movement and action—gestures are not sufficient. A glove puppet is not restricted by leg movements and can cross from place to place with the utmost speed and flexibility. Players should take advantage of this to keep plenty of action in their plays. If a play is to be performed before a selected audience all concerned with the play

Class Production, and Stories Suitable for Plays

should aim to do their best, but it must be well remembered, by those in charge, that the standard set must be within the scope of the players.

Certain puppets lend themselves to different kinds of plays. Gloves are excellent for fun, and are sure to be a success if allowed to carry, embrace, push and pull, fight, dance and go in and out of doors carrying various articles, which can be carefully placed on to the playboard. Rod puppets are good for serious drama and can be dignified even when called upon to fight with swords. String puppets can climb and swing, dance and perform any amount of tricks, while shadows are delightful for fantasy and dreams, poetry and songs.

For various reasons it may be desirable to have all the children in a class taking an active interest in the production, and there are various ways to cope with a large number.

1. The teacher may allow the children to choose three or four plays to act, then divide his class into three or four groups and let each group be responsible for the production of one play.

2. He may let the children choose one story to dramatise and this can be discussed by the whole class. The class can then be divided into groups, and each group must decide the form the play will take. The groups rehearse their version of the story, and eventually act the play to the other children, when, under the teacher's guidance, much useful criticism can be heard.

3. One play is chosen but each character has several manipulators who take turns with the puppets.

4. One play only is selected and then the children are asked to volunteer to become scene painters, scene shifters, property managers, wardrobe mistresses, etc. etc. In this way all the children can be absorbed into the production, but care should be taken to give these children credit on the day of the performance.

Spontaneous dialogue is very necessary and below is a list of situations which give opportunities for this.

1. A lady asks another the way to a shop or to the park.
2. A boy finds a lost dog and takes him to a policeman.
3. The doctor visits a patient, and the mother talks to him.
4. Two mothers talk about their children and their school work.
5. A mother and a child go shopping.

6. A mother tells a child to go to bed and he does not want to go.
7. A boy throws a stone and it breaks a window. He goes to the house to apologise.
8. Two puppets carry on a telephone conversation.
9. Puppets discuss a popular film being shown in the neighbourhood.
10. One puppet asks another what he thinks of a certain programme on the T.V.
11. Puppets discuss their favourite actor or actress.

Nursery rhymes are always excellent material for puppet plays and there are various ways of using them.

1. The teacher can manipulate the puppets while the children sing or recite the rhyme.
2. Each child can hold a puppet and recite a rhyme, performing actions to fit the words.
3. A nursery rhyme can be made into a story and puppets can become the characters of the story.

Practically all *folk stories* can be made into plays and the animal ones are especially suitable for YOUNG CHILDREN, as also are the repetitive ones.

The Three Bears.
The Three Pigs.
Red Riding Hood.
Billy Goat Gruff.
Peter Rabbit.
Elves and the Shoe Maker.
Chicken Licken.

Wise Old Goat.
The Old Woman and the Fox.
Little Red Hen.
Mother Hubbard.
Brer Rabbit.
Snow White and the Seven Dwarfs.

STORIES SUITABLE FOR CHILDREN OF JUNIOR AGE

Robin Hood.
Aesop's Fables.
St. George and the Dragon.
Little Black Sambo.
Rumpelstiltskin.
Hans Andersen's Stories.
Grimm's Stories.

Cinderella.
William Tell.
Ali Baba and the Forty Thieves.
Beauty and the Beast.
Jack and the Beanstalk.
The Three Wishes.

King of the Golden River.
Just So Stories.
The Shepherdess and the
  Chimney Sweep.
Hansel and Gretel.
Dick Whittington.

King Midas.
The Pied Piper.
Hiawatha.
Sir Eglamore.
Winnie the Pooh.

STORIES SUITABLE FOR SENIORS

St. George and the Dragon.
Greek Myths.
Selections from
  Alice in Wonderland.
Just So Stories.
Sleeping Beauty.
Aladdin.
Robinson Crusoe.
Rip van Winkle.
Treasure Island.

Selections from *Oliver Twist.*
Selections from
  Uncle Tom's Cabin.
Arabian Nights
  Entertainments.
Willow Pattern Plate Story.
Sinbad the Sailor.
Don Quixote.
Beowulf.
Scenes from Shakespeare.

Boys enjoy making an animal puppet *orchestra*, each animal having a musical instrument and making his own characteristic noise. Excellent for string puppets. Girls enjoy dressing puppets in traditional national costumes, and these puppets can be made to dance most realistically. Rod or glove puppets should be used.

STORIES WITH A HISTORY BIAS

Tales of King Arthur and
  his Knights.
Queen Elizabeth and
  Sir Francis Drake.
Guy Fawkes.

King Alfred and the Cakes.
Two Pilgrim Fathers.
Florence Nightingale.
Joan of Arc.

Mock tournaments, using rod puppets, and conflicts between men and animals make good puppet material.

BIBLE STORIES

The Christmas Story.
Story of Ruth.

Paul and Silas in Prison.
Abraham and Isaac.

Joseph in Prison.
David and Goliath.
Samuel and Eli.
Moses in the Bulrushes.
Jonah and the Whale.

Rescue of St. Paul.
The Good Samaritan.
Scenes from
    The Pilgrim's Progress.

APPROPRIATE MUSIC TO USE WITH PUPPET PLAYS

Toy Symphony	*Haydn*
Nut Cracker Suite	*Tschaikovsky*
Dance Caprice	*Grieg*
Minute Valse	*Chopin*
Mother Goose Suite	*Ravel*
Kinder Symphonie	*Haydn*
Elfentanz	*Grieg*

The following instruments are useful for local atmosphere: Drums for jungle scenes, tambourines for Spanish scenes and banjos for South American.

EFFECTS FOR PLAYS

Lightning is made by flashing the lights on and off.

Thunder is produced by shaking a piece of sheet tin.

Rain is made by filling a biscuit tin full of beans and moving the box slowly in a rotating manner.

Fire. Place a red electric light bulb behind a set of miniature logs to get this effect. Augment if desired with a red spotlight.

Revolver shot. A yard stick against the floor makes this noise.

Crash of china. To create this illusion fill a wooden box with old crockery, glass and a few stones. Nail a top to the box and tip it from end to end.

Train. Partially fill a small metal box with small tacks, and if these are shaken in jerks it sounds like a train starting from a station.

Horses. Take two halves of a coconut and clap them on a piece of heavy wood, making the sound of horses' hooves.

VIII: Puppetry Linked to Other Subjects in the Curriculum

It is impossible to give definite rules whereby a teacher can link puppetry, in a formal manner, with the other subjects in the school, for children's interests arise from various stimulations and the situations in the classrooms are never the same. I can, however, give suggestions regarding the work and I am sure that each individual teacher will see the possibilities of using the ideas in his own environment. I will discuss working both with the younger and the older children.

If a child is to read well he must be able to speak well, and there is no better way of procuring free, natural, fluent speech than by letting a child express himself freely without supervision with a puppet. The puppet assumes all the characteristics, and the desirable and undesirable traits, that the child wills, and he becomes a trusted friend to whom even a shy child will talk freely given the opportunity to indulge in such freedom. After this spontaneous playing a child who cannot read should be encouraged to draw and paint about his puppet interest, the teacher writing the words describing his pictures beneath and beside his illustrations. The child gradually learns to copy the letters, and to associate certain groupings of letters with certain drawings. When the child can recognise some of the words there is no necessity for the teacher to write directly on to the child's drawing paper, but, instead, to write on separate cards for the child to use when he needs a copy. As the child progresses to the writing of sentences the teacher will find it a good idea to let him keep a small special notebook in which to refer to those sentences and words he knows best and needs most.

Older children should be encouraged to make reference books and give the books titles, e.g. "My puppet book" or "How I make my puppets". In these books the children can record how they made their puppets, how they used them, any conversations and plays in which the puppets took a part, in fact anything to do with their puppets. Not only will these books be records of a child's active work, but the child will frequently read them, as the contents are of personal interest to him, and by so doing he gets the constant reading practice he needs. As the puppet interest spreads throughout the class a teacher would be wise to make attractive reference books to hang on the walls in positions easy for a child to reach and use. These books should contain all the words in alphabetical order that a child is likely to need when he is writing about puppets. Other books should show clearly various methods of making puppets, while others should contain patterns for the gloves and suggestions for dressing. Because the children have a desire to use these books it is usually only a short step to the memorising of the words through use and copying. Words become sentences, sentences become stories and stories become plays ready to be acted. Sometimes a child can create a story, but he is not sufficiently advanced to write it down. When such a case arises give this child an opportunity of telling his story to others, for not only will this clarify it in his own mind, but his tale may appeal to other children who may be prepared to help him put it down on paper.

It must be remembered that it is important to let a child tell his story without interruptions. To stop spontaneous speech in order to correct speech may make a child entirely lose the thread of his story, or a child will not tell his story if he fears that his teacher will use him as an example of how *not* to talk. The teacher should note the mistakes and allocate a time for a class lesson on the subject of clear speech, etc. There are, too, some children who long to tell a story, but are not creative themselves; and these children should be encouraged to tell and write the simple folk stories which are ideal for puppet plays. Many of the infant reading primers contain excellent material for plays for children of all ages.

It is easier to make a success of a puppet play if the puppets are actually on the hands, so as soon as a child has a play ready let him experiment with puppets. It is amusing to watch how the children add to the dialogue and improve it at each successive dramatic session. This free acting can go on for quite a long time without special help from an adult, but eventually the children will want to give a performance to others and will consult the teacher regarding the production. If the performance is to be given to other children I do not think that the players

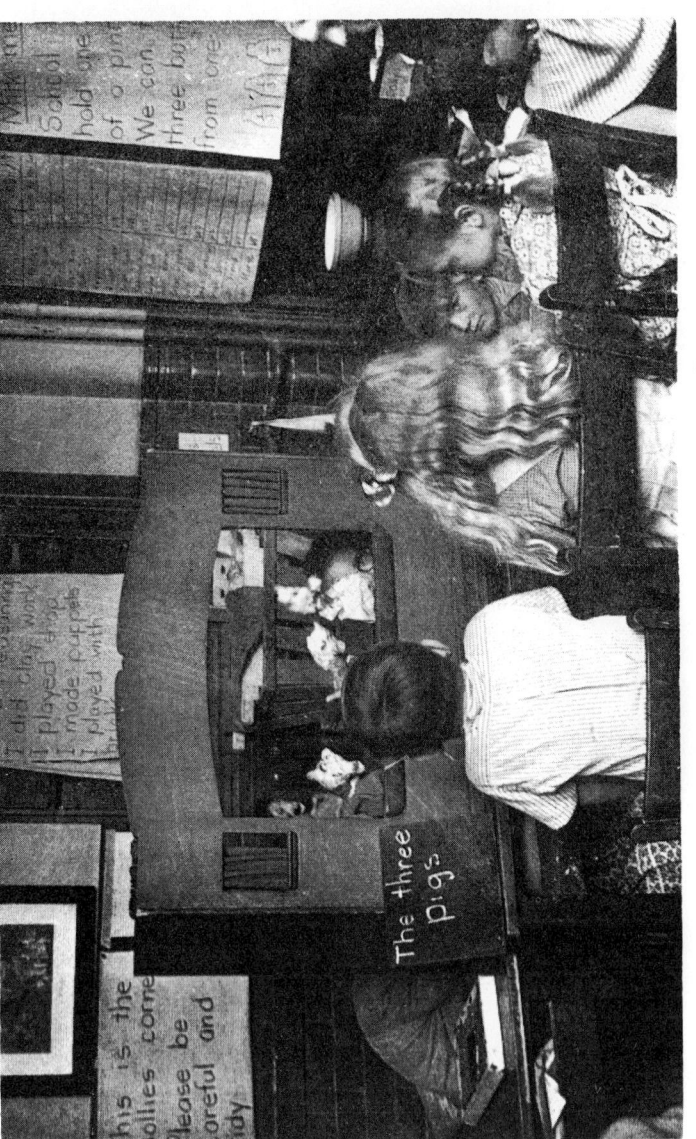

Spontaneous classroom acting using a small stage

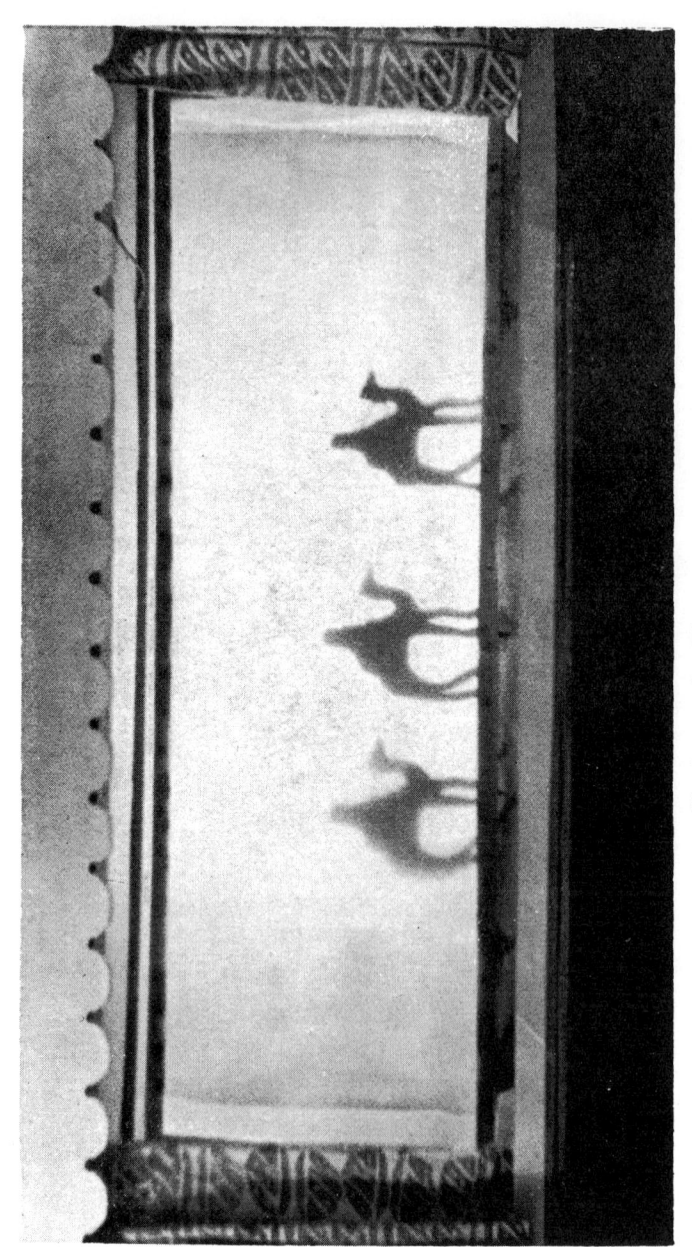

Shadows—the Three Wise Men

String puppets made by juniors

Puppets from Hiawatha. Back-cloth painted by children with powder paint on cotton material

Acting in the playground

Stage improvised from a clothes-horse (the play is The Owl and The Pussy-cat*)*

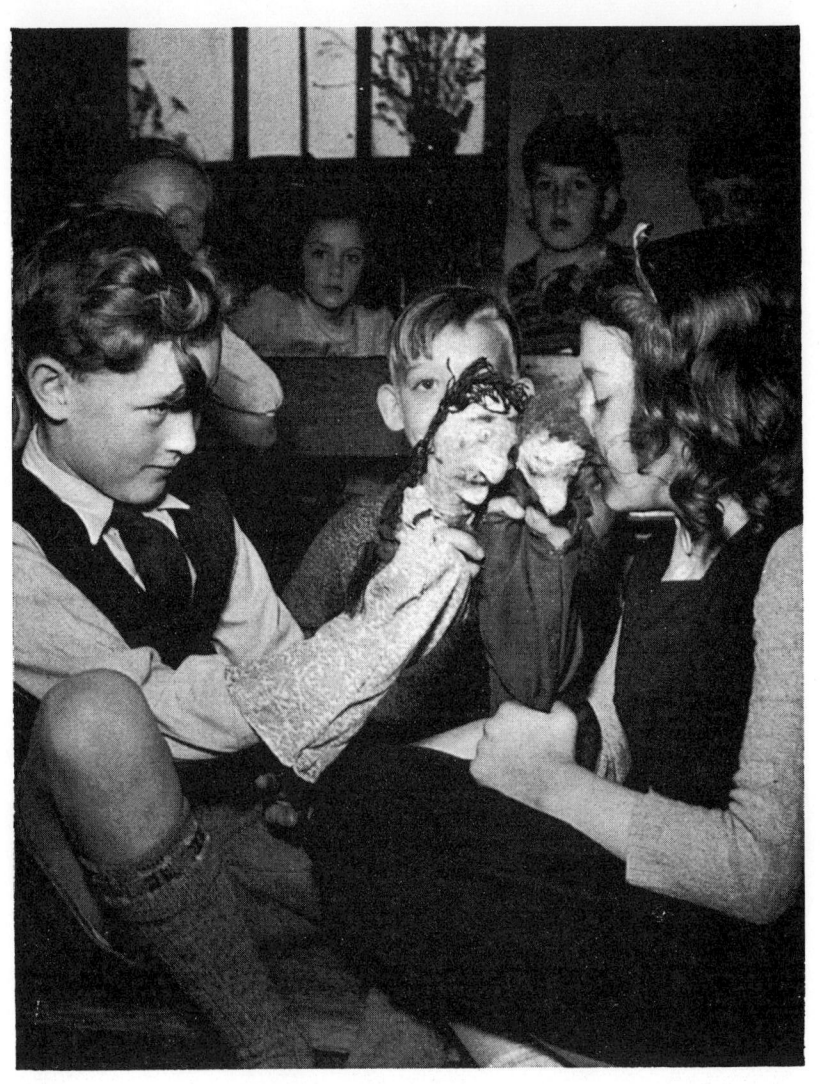

Spontaneous classroom acting

A shadow puppet show

need to perfect all the manipulation, for children seem to understand each other, and the ideas expressed need little explanation. On the other hand if adults are to be invited to the performance I think it is wise for the teacher to explain to the children involved the necessity for proper rehearsals, as grown-ups expect more polished productions and should not be invited unless the children are prepared to give their time and work to the best of their abilities.

Care should be taken to see that the effort and time given to a finished production do not exceed the educational value of the result obtained. It should be explained to the children that, although it is fun to improvise during free acting, it is not fair to do this when a performance has a time limit, and definite dialogue. Each character is waiting for a certain cue, and a play can be completely ruined by someone who has an unexpected brainwave on the night.

Returning to the question of child audiences, I used to find it a good idea to allow each child concerned with a puppet play to invite one friend from any other class to make up the audience, for I found that the children sometimes liked to show off to their older and younger friends. Nevertheless a teacher may find it easier to organise if he invites a complete class to see the play, but the circumstances depend upon the amount of disciplined freedom in the school as a whole.

The handwriting of the stories seems to give some teachers anxiety. If children are creatively writing it is sometimes wise not to be too critical regarding the formation of the letters, for children's thoughts often flow more quickly forward than their pencils, which are slow for lack of skill. The urge to put down on to paper any imaginative ideas should not be stifled simply because a child misspells or writes badly. If a story is good let the teacher praise it, and suggest that it is rewritten clearly so that others can also enjoy reading it. A performance given to an audience is an excellent excuse for writing practice. The invitations to the show can be examples of the best writing, and the pictures advertising or describing it can be painted and well printed. Children, not particularly interested in the making of puppets, are nevertheless often interested and keen to help with the art, and I know of one case where there was so much enthusiasm that the teacher suggested that all the puppet pictures should be displayed in the classroom as an exhibition for all to see. There are always certain children who are happy to write and make the admission tickets.

Let us presume that it is decided that a performance is to be given and the children wish to discuss the stage. Previously they may have been content to act behind a blackboard or a screen, but they will realise that something more ambitious is required for public entertainment. A group of children should be responsible for this and ideas collected from all. According to the ages of the children, so the degrees of skill in making will vary. Small children will probably nail together laths to make a wooden screen, or have two orange boxes on one side and two on the other with a curtain across; but the older children attending woodwork classes will want to make something more lasting. Whatever method or skill is used the materials must be purchased or procured. The former is excellent, for this means a visit to a shop where the children can be responsible for the monies and the checking of any change. The lengths of wood must be carefully measured and it is obvious that the making of the stage can be a practical number interest.

Another group of children can sew the curtains and these can be decorated with embroidery, potato prints, lino prints, or any other bold decoration designed by the children. Some will want to draw, colour and design the back-cloths or make the properties. Then there is always the older boy who adores anything electrical, and will joyfully spend his time setting up the lights and effects, especially if he is allowed to use his own initiative when organising the wiring of the stage for the lights, and the working of them. In my experience, this particular type of child often seems to have a father who is also interested in electricity, and the child is proud to discuss his problems at home; with the result that there is co-operation between the school and the home. Children of this type become a part of the production and gain enormously given these opportunities of leadership.

The number interest returns with the discussion on tickets. Are tickets necessary and if so, what shall be their size and what shall they cost? If a money charge is to be made (young children often use paper money) certain children should organise the charges and give a definite and careful account of the takings and expenses. It is not always necessary to have money for the charge. I knew a class of children who decided that everyone desirous of coming to their show should recite a short poem or a nursery

Puppetry Linked to Other Subjects in the Curriculum 67

rhyme as a charge, and the results were hilarious. Fortunately the actual puppet play only lasted fifteen minutes, so there was ample time to enjoy each new arrival, especially when he set himself out to be amusing.

Seating accommodation sets another arithmetical problem. How many chairs can occupy a certain area? How will they be arranged so that all can see? Obviously the children must measure the chairs and the floor space to find out the answers, or they may find the room unpleasantly crowded.

Opportunities to practise other subjects arise unexpectedly, as in the case when certain children chose the story of the Gingerbread Boy for a shadow play. It was discovered that some of the children had no idea what gingerbread was. The teacher brought to school a simple recipe and the ingredients were weighed and mixed in the classroom, rolled and shaped into gingerbread boys, baked in the oven in the staffroom, and finally eaten with great delight by the children. Not only did the making involve the weighing of all the ingredients but also the writing of the recipe, the use of reference books to gain information regarding ginger, and of course the usual descriptive work in the children's work books. In addition when the puppets were being made, it was decided that the animals must be of certain sizes, so the rulers were much used for this active work, as too, were the reference books again, to discover the shapes and habits of the animals.

A teacher should be ready to follow any lead or interest which may arise from any of his work. For example, a teacher interested in puppetry had shown her children how to make puppets, and after discussion it was decided that each child should make an animal. Quite apart from the puppets a great interest in animals was stimulated, and many children not making puppets nevertheless wanted to know more about the animals. Being an intelligent woman, the teacher did not miss the opportunity given her, and she continued the work by helping the children to discover all the information they desired. She also obtained good books containing animal stories, encouraged the children to make up their own stories about animals, and she increased their vocabularies by making books to hang on the walls which contained words of reference, e.g. names of animals and their young—words such as "Herds of cows"—"gaggle of geese", etc.

It is unwise to introduce poetry into a puppet play unless it arises naturally, and then the children should be allowed to use it. There are, of course, some poems which dramatise more suitably than others, but it is extremely easy to lose the feeling of a poem. I have seen both *Hiawatha* and *The Pied Piper* admirably adapted, and in both cases the plays arose from a love of the poems. The stories of the poems were made into plays by the children in their own words with a great deal of humour, but the beautiful descriptive portions were learnt by the whole class and recited in chorus by children grouped at the side fronts of the stage.

Musical children, uninterested in hand-work, can often be brought in to help with the puppet play when asked to suggest or select the music needed for accompaniments and interludes. Sometimes it is possible to form a group who are willing to rehearse with recorders and other instruments, and who are willing to help behind the scenes with incidental music when required.

Children painting the scenery should be given scope for their talents, and be allowed to evolve their own ideas and use their own mediums. If the play is set in a foreign country they will probably need to use reference books, to discover certain data, in order to satisfy the puppeteers who have entrusted the work to them. For instance, a play set in Switzerland may need scenery with mountains, chalets and people in national dress; or a play set in another period may need detailed knowledge of costumes and furniture. Reading around a subject is of the utmost importance, for anything that creates an interest in books should be encouraged. I have known children, after reading around their subject, decide to completely alter their play, because while looking for certain facts they have found something more interesting to dramatise. A teacher has to use his own discretion when such cases arise, but unless it is of importance to finish the original play, I feel he should allow the new interest to flourish, for it means that the children have read with understanding.

Puppetry can be used by the teacher to emphasise historical facts. A well-known puppeteer in Amiens gives performances to children, and one of his methods is to choose personalities from history and make them the centres of his "lessons". He first shows a puppet whom he calls Guignol, and this puppet enters and explains to the audience of children what is going to happen. He holds up certain objects and also shows the children cards on which are written words connected with the personality; and

Puppetry Linked to Other Subjects in the Curriculum 69

from these clues the children guess the individual. When the central figure is discovered a puppet is shown who resembles, as far as possible, this historical person and who is dressed in the costume of the period. The children are encouraged to ask this puppet any questions they wish, e.g. the person to be discovered might be Jeanne D'Arc. Music is played, "il était une bergère" and a sheep passes in front of a card bearing the word "Domrémy". Other cards bear the words Reims, Charles VII; Chinon-Orléans-Compiègne-Rouen; 1412-1431. When the children have discovered the identity, the puppet appears as Jeanne D'Arc. Often Guignol reappears and helps in the discussion, talking with Jeanne and giving the children a lead for their questions, and it is a lively lesson in history and satisfies the curiosity.

Many children are now taught French in school and it is sometimes difficult to make the children converse. The master should enlist the help of puppets, for often the children will make their puppets talk French when they will not exchange the same sentences with another child. It makes a variation if the teacher sometimes uses puppets for the practice of verbs or the introduction of grammar. A puppet can be made to repeat anything, and if necessary the puppet can be singularly stupid so that the rule, etc., can be explained to him again and again slowly and carefully. All this is good for the slower and less able child, for it gives him a chance to learn at the same slow pace without feeling backward, while the quick child can use a "bright" puppet.

I suppose it is obvious that the opportunities for teaching needlework are many when the children begin to dress their puppets. Both boys and girls should be encouraged to make their own paper patterns, to find the materials on which to place the patterns, and to cut them out. They can join the seams together with simple stitches, and learn the embroidery stitches when they decorate the glove. A glove puppet is so small that even a young child can finish the task without undue fatigue, and the joy is great when the finished garment is finally fitted to the head.

This chapter would not be complete unless I mentioned the beneficial effects that arise when children with emotional difficulties use puppets. Children need to dramatise the grown-up world in order to understand it, and they need to play out their experiences. By familiarising their fears they no longer fear them, and again and again I have seen a child's own frustrations and troubles transferred to his puppets. I've been able, too, to help a child, simply by watching and listening to him as he uses his puppet, for, by his unfettered conversation, he has unconsciously given me a clue to his behaviour problems. Stammerers can often be helped by using puppets and it was an amazing experience for me when I invited one to come behind a puppet screen. Her speech was appallingly tied up and it was difficult for her to say one sentence without a struggle. I thought the experience might be something of a treat for her, but to my surprise, with a puppet on her hand, she repeated a complete poem without hesitation. Later, she would also join in some of the puppet plays, but she herself always had to be well screened before she spoke clearly. Nevertheless with practice with puppets there was a definite improvement in her everyday speech.

The puppet stage is a great joy to the shy, the clumsy, the plain and the deformed, for all these children have opportunities to take the star parts when acting in a puppet play. They are not often picked for parts in the ordinary dramatic productions for obvious reasons, but how often must they long to be chosen. Behind the screen with a puppet on their hand they can become the most beautiful princesses and the most dashing princes.

I hope this chapter has shown the great usefulness of puppetry in school, and in conclusion I should like to emphasise that it also strengthens confidences, calls for initiative, and encourages team work in addition to drawing certain school subjects together.

IX: Short Account of Puppetry in Other Countries

PUNCH

IT is interesting to trace the familiar character of Punch, and find his counterpart in almost every country except America. In England he is known as Punch, in France Polichinelle, in Italy as Pulcinello, in Germany as Kasper, in Turkey as Karagheuz, in India as Viduska, in Persia as Ketschel, in Russia as Petroushka. The same characteristics are found in each country; the hook nose and the mischievous nature. In order to produce the strange voice of Punch the performer fixes a contrivance in his mouth which alters his natural speaking voice.

COUNTRIES OF THE WESTERN WORLD

The puppet theatres of Western Europe can now be roughly grouped into two categories, folk and art. The traditional dramas and primitive figures are presented in the former and these can be found in certain parts of France, Belgium, Germany, Italy, Sicily and Greece. In general all the folk theatres represent dying traditions, and these are only kept alive by intellectual enthusiasts; and in spite of this they may disappear, for on the whole they no longer appeal to the working-class audiences for whom they were originally created. The second category consists of art theatres used by gifted professional puppeteers who give brilliant performances regularly in their own theatres, and these theatres often have excellent museums attached to them.

England

In England puppetry flourished in Shakespeare's time and could be seen at most country fairs. When the Puritans shut down the legitimate stage in 1642 the puppet shows were permitted to continue. Samuel Pepys wrote in 1667 that he went to Bartholomew's Fair and found Lady Castlemaine at a puppet play called *Patient Grizill*. He also mentions that he saw the tale of "Whittington" as a puppet show as well as an Italian play in the same year. In the eighteenth century Boswell tells us a story about Oliver Goldsmith nearly breaking his leg trying to prove that he could jump over a broomstick as gracefully as a puppet! Over the years puppetry has continued to be popular with a certain section of the population and there are many professional and amateur puppeteers in England. The majority of these, however, have no special theatres, but give performances, many of a very high standard, to various audiences in hired halls: or carry their own portable stages to their various engagements. One puppeteer has, however, with great initiative, succeeded in founding a permanent puppet theatre—the Little Angel—in Islington, London, and there it is possible to see excellent professional productions. Television has brought puppetry to many who would otherwise not have been familiar with the medium, and it is used in many children's programmes.

Sicily

The Sicilian puppet is large and heavy, generally constructed of solid wood, jointed with metal joints and manipulated with two heavy iron rods, one running through the top of the head and the other to the right hand which holds the sword; the left hand is manipulated by a string. One of the most famous plays depicts the marvellous prowess of Orlando; and Roland, one of the twelve peers of King Charlemagne, was the prototype of Orlando. The plays centring on Orlando are derived from Ariosto's epic poem, Orlando Furioso, and many are still being played in Sicily.

America

Probably the first puppets in America were used by the Indians in their religious rites. The secrets of their manipulation were carefully guarded, and it was believed by the audience that the figures were granted the gift of life by means of the Great Spirit entering the body of the tribal medicine man. Now, throughout the country, puppetry is a universally accepted form of entertain-

Short Account of Puppetry in Other Countries

ment, and there are numbers of professional and amateur puppeteers using glove, rod, string, and shadow puppets. As in England it is extensively used in the schools.

EASTERN EUROPE AND ASIA

Russia

Russian puppetry is now famous all over the world, and rightly so, because of the high standard of the productions. Both professional and amateur companies flourish in most cities and all are given encouragement by the State. It is also used to spread Soviet ideas, and it is widely used in the education of the people. In the cities there are specially built puppet theatres and the performances provide excellent entertainment for children and adults. Behind the scenes there may be as many as ten or twenty manipulators, and one production may use as many as thirty staff.

Czecho-Slovakia

Czecho-Slovakia has had a puppet tradition for many centuries and still continues to produce some of the best puppets and puppeteers. Provision is made for the systematic training of puppet artists by the State, and courses are organised at district, regional and national levels.

Poland

. Poland is yet another country with state-aided puppet theatres, and there are some excellent shows to be seen in her principal towns.

Persia

Legend has it that centuries ago in Persia puppets were extremely popular, and the soldiers took their favourite ones to war with them. In time they became a part of the Secret Service, because these puppets could be passed between the enemy's lines, and it was possible for a spy in the enemy camp to secrete his information by this means!

Java

The Javanese are Mohammedan by faith, and are therefore restricted from making figures representing the human form, because on the Day of Judgement every image maker must provide the images he has made with a soul. This probably accounts for the grotesque and bizarre shapes of their puppets. The Javanese theatre, or form of theatre, was called the "Wayang", and developed through various stages. The oldest form of dramatic entertainment in Java was the shadow play, the Wayang Beber and the Wayang Purwa. The former had scenes painted on long sheets of cloth or paper, and seven of these rolls were passed across the screen for each performance, which lasted from one to one and a half hours. The story was recited by a speaker and was usually concerned with the exploits of Pandji. This was once a popular entertainment, but it has slowly died out. The more popular Wayang Purwa had puppets cut out of water buffalo hide with strange profiles and long thin arms, and hands which were manipulated by rods made of horn. Men were allowed to see the manipulation of the puppets, but the women were only allowed to see the shadows.

Another form of play was the Wayang Kiltik, and for this the puppets were carved in soft wood with a flat form, and each side of the wood was carved in relief, with the arms of leather worked by rods. These puppets were not used as shadows, but were seen by an audience of men. The next form of entertainment, the Wayang Golek, had puppets of wood, but these were carved in the round with movable heads and arms and completely costumed; they were manipulated like the others, from beneath with rods. Following on from the Kiltik was the Wayang Topeng, and living actors were masked and dressed to imitate the puppets, the masks being made of skin and wood. The spoken parts were all taken by one man called a "Dalang", and the performance was accompanied by an orchestra of native instruments, the performers imitating the conventionalised dance patterns of the puppets. Yet another form was the Wayang Redok, where the actors gave up the mask, and painted features on to their own faces and spoke their own parts. This last step was mainly in the nineteenth century and was probably caused by the influence of European civilisation. Most of the types of plays can be found in Java in certain villages, but definitely the most popular is the Wayang

Short Account of Puppetry in Other Countries

Purwa, the straight shadow play which takes for its theme the story from Mahabharata and the Ramayana, for in this story can be found adventure, romance and religion. Three characters in the Hindu epic are Petruk, Gareng and Semar, but Semar is sometimes the father of Petruk and Gareng. These true native characters seem to satisfy the Javanese desire for the ridiculous and the sublime.

There are two main types of Javanese shadow puppets. One has a thin nose and slant eyes which are supposed to indicate wisdom and high rank, and the other has a short nose, round brow, round eyes and a broad mouth said to indicate power and strength. Gods are invisible and are therefore always dressed in black, as this colour is the colour of invisibility. They are the only shadow puppets to wear shoes, for Gods are not of this earth and their feet must not touch the ground.

PART TWO

PUPPET PLAYS WRITTEN AND ACTED BY CHILDREN

X: The Circus Rehearsal

A play for glove puppets

This particular play arose directly from a class interest in the making of puppets, and was performed with much success at a Craft Exhibition at the County Hall, London. The puppets were not made with a story in mind, and were consequently very varied. When a large group of children wanted to use their puppets, it was decided to make up a play about a circus, in order to bring in all the characters. After a great deal of discussion the children called their play *A Circus Rehearsal*, because they wished to include some of their mistakes which they thought were funny. To shorten the play exclude some of the "acts".

The play should be played with speed with no waits between speeches and with plenty of action.

CHARACTERS

RINGMASTER. He was complete with black top hat, red felt coat, gay waistcoat; the concealing glove was black. He carried a long whip, had a big moustache, and a large tooth sticking out of the front of his mouth. (Upon enquiring the nature of the substance of the tooth, I discovered that it had lately fallen from the owner's own mouth!)

SYLVIA, the beautiful horse rider. She was blonde, and wore a very full lace skirt which flowed over the horse and made it look as if she were really riding the horse.

HORSE. He was made from a Vim tin, his head was of papier mâché, his mane was a fringe, his tail a tassel, his reins and accoutrements made from felt and braid. He was operated by a rod fixed in the Vim tin.

FOUR CLOWNS. One of the clowns did not have a fixed head, and a piece of dowelling was put through the tube of his neck so that he was able to elongate his neck, or twist his head round at will.

Boy
Magician
Tiger
Danny the Dog
Freddy Fox
Freda Fox
Uncle Harry—the conjurer
Rabbit (white or pink)
Baggy Pants
Porky Pig
Pinky Pig

PROPERTIES

Piece of cord about 6 in. long
Toy watering can
Small bowl
Carrot
Tennis ball, painted and fixed to a stick
Foot rule
Four 1 in. bricks
A cardboard top hat with the back cut away, and of a size to rest on the playing shelf
Doll's house
Pot of flowers—or a bunch of flowers
Artificial bubble maker. This can be bought at any trick shop
Five 1 in. beads threaded on to a piece of cord about 6 in. long
Short stick for a puppet to hold
One 3 in. cube or box

SCENE

The interior of a circus.

(Ringmaster enters and addresses the audience.)

Ringmaster: Ladies and Gentlemen, you are about to see a rehearsal of a circus performance. Please remember that it is only a rehearsal and the turns may not be perfect. First come the clowns.

The Circus Rehearsal

(Exit Ringmaster.)
(Enter 1st Clown.)

1st Clown: Watch me tumble. *(He rolls sidewards and backwards along the playboard (the top shelf) laughing and talking as he pleases. He stops and goes centre front to talk to the audience).*

1st Clown: I forgot to tell you that my name is Poko, and I love being a clown. The trouble is that so many boys try to be clowns *(pause)*—at the wrong time—at least, so our teacher says *(a boy enters from side)*. Now here's a boy, and I wouldn't mind betting that he wants to be a clown. Well, Boy, what is it?

Boy: I want to be a clown.

1st Clown *(to audience)*: What did I tell you? *(To Boy.)* Before you can be a clown you must learn to tumble.

Boy: All right, I'll try. *(He tries to tumble and makes a hopeless mess of it, bumping his head, etc. etc.)*

1st Clown: You can't tumble so you can't be a clown. *(The Boy begins to cry loudly, and then the Clown cries too. Up springs a Magician from below stage.)*

Magician: What a shocking row. Stop it and tell me the trouble. *(They stop crying.)*

1st Clown *(to audience)*: It's the Magician!
(To Magician): This Boy wants to be a clown, and he can't tumble.

Magician: Come here, Boy. *(Boy moves to Magician.)* Are you sure that you want to be a clown?

Boy: Oh yes, please.

Magician: Stand still. *(He waves his wand over the boy and says)* Mumble jumble tumble tumble, mumble jumble tumble tumble. Be a Clown!
(Immediately the Boy drops below the stage, and a clown puppet with a similar face takes his place.)

Boy now 2nd Clown: Hurrah, hurrah, I'm a clown! Let's see if I can tumble. *(He proceeds to tumble and roll correctly while the 1st Clown claps and encourages him. The Magician vanishes below. Enter 3rd Clown carrying a cord. Enter 4th Clown with the detachable neck who does all the tricks he can manage for the audience's benefit. While this is going on the 1st and 3rd Clowns are moving about and each takes an end of the cord.)*

1st Clown: Who would like to skip?

2ND CLOWN: I can't skip, but I would like to swing. (*He sits on the cord while the 1st and 3rd Clowns gently swing him, counting at the same time from 1 to 6. When they get to 6 they swing high, and the 2nd Clown is thrown on to the playing board. With exclamations of distress, the clowns gather round the 2nd Clown.*)

1ST CLOWN: I think that he is dead.

3RD CLOWN: No, he's not. You watch me revive him. (*He goes off stage while the others talk freely. The 3rd Clown returns with a watering can and he pours water all over the 2nd Clown, who jumps up.*)

2ND CLOWN: Stop it. You are making me all wet.

4TH CLOWN: Anyway, you are better. (*The Clowns jump, twist and turn about stage.*)

CURTAIN DOWN

ACT TWO

(*The Ringmaster looks through the curtains—centre.*)

RINGMASTER: Now you will see a ferocious tiger.

CURTAIN UP

(*Enter a Tiger who wanders up and down stage. He turns to the audience.*)

TIGER: I'm not really ferocious. I'm really very kind, but I get so hungry I could eat anything. When I am hungry I try to go to sleep and forget about food. You won't mind if I do my act later, will you? (*He goes to sleep.*)

Danny the Dog looks round the corner of the stage. He comes a little way on and then stops.)

DANNY: I'm glad the Tiger isn't here, for when he is hungry he says he will eat me.

(*With his head down Danny begins to sniff around. He sniffs up the curtain and around the bottom of it. Gradually with his head down he sniffs along the playing board (or "playboard") without looking up at all, until he suddenly finds himself pushing his nose into the Tiger. The Tiger wakes up with a yell.*)

The Circus Rehearsal

TIGER: You have woken me up so now I shall eat you. (*He begins to chase the dog round and round the stage, until suddenly Danny stops and faces the tiger.*)
DANNY: Pax, pax, I give in and I am sorry that I woke you up. Please don't eat me.
TIGER (*He comes to front, puts his paws on to the playing board and hangs his head*): I'm so very hungry.
DANNY: I'll find you something to eat. (*He goes off and returns with a large carrot.*)
TIGER: That's no good to me. (*He starts to chase the dog, who runs off stage, but returns carrying a large bowl which he places on the playing board.*)
This looks better. (*He puts his head into it and eats.*)
Now I feel strong enough to show you all how I turn a heavy ball. (*He places the tennis ball on to the shelf and then he orders it to move or stop.*)
DANNY: That's a good circus trick. I'd like to try that. (*He goes up to the ball and in doing so he exposes the stick on which it is fixed and moved from below.*)
What a cunning trick!
TIGER: Oh dear, everyone will know how the trick is done now. (*He chases the dog off stage.*)

CURTAIN DOWN

ACT THREE

The foot ruler and the four 1 in. bricks should be placed at one end of the playing board.

CURTAIN UP

(*Enter Freddy and Freda Fox. They each bow to the audience and then they solemnly bow to each other. They pick up the foot rule one at each end, and show it to the audience.*)
FREDDY: Ladies and Gentlemen, this is a foot.
(*Enter 1st Clown at back stage.*)
1ST CLOWN: Funny sort of foot. I'd like to see someone walk on that. Perhaps it is a crutch. (*He pretends to limp across the stage.*)

FREDDY: If you were to go to school you would learn about these feet.

1ST CLOWN: First you say it is a "foot" and now you say it is "feet". Make up your mind, Freddy.

FREDDY: Be quiet or go away. (*Clown goes.*) Freda, how many inches in this foot?

FREDA: Twelve.

FREDDY: Good girl. Now let us measure this stage. (*Taking an end each they measure.*) It's two feet six inches. (*They put the ruler away.*)

FREDA: Let us count the bricks.

(*Freda carries one brick from end of the playing shelf to the other, and says "one". Freddy carries another and says "two". They turn to get the remaining bricks and while their backs are turned the Clown takes one brick away. Freddy and Freda bring two more bricks and say "three" and "four".*)

FREDDY (*looking at the bricks*): I thought we had four bricks but there are only three here.

FREDA: We did have four. We must go and look for the other one before we begin our trick.

(*While they are looking for the missing brick, the Clown, without being seen by them, replaces it.*)

FREDA: You must have counted wrongly. I'm going to count again. (*She touches each brick and counts.*) One, two, three, four. Really, Freddy, you are being rather silly. (*She goes over to him, and while she does this the Clown removes another brick.*)

FREDDY (*He goes over to the bricks and counts*): One, two, three. Freda, you are wrong, there are only three bricks. (*This placing, counting, taking and replacing goes on for as long as desired, the Clown nearly getting caught as he makes the changes. Child audiences greatly enjoy this particular entertainment, and often enter into the fun by calling to the foxes or the clown.*)

FREDDY: I'm fed up with this. I'm going to see the Ringmaster.

FREDA: I think we ought to see the shop steward.

FREDDY: A good idea. We will. (*Exeunt foxes.*)

(*Enter the Clown.*)

CLOWN (*He walks up and down front stage*): Ha, ha, ha, ha.

CURTAIN DOWN

ACT FOUR

(*The Ringmaster parts the centre curtains and speaks to the audience.*)

RINGMASTER: No performance is complete without a conjurer, and so I shall now introduce our conjurer who is called—Uncle Harry.

CURTAIN UP

(*Uncle Harry comes on carrying a top hat which can be made of paper. The back of the hat is cut away but the audience cannot see this. He places the hat on the playing shelf.*)

CONJURER (*He speaks to the audience*): Ladies and Gentlemen, you see before you an ordinary hat, but my magic will bring forth wonderful objects. (*He waves his wand over the hat, at the same time saying*):
Rappity frappity come up flowers.
(*Slowly a pot or bunch of flowers emerges at the top of the hat (it has been pushed up from below) and the Conjurer takes them and shows them to the audience, at the same time bowing. He places the flowers on the playing board. He returns to the hat and again waves his wand.*)
Rappity frappity come up rabbit.
(*At the top of the hat appears a rabbit, and he stays there cleaning his whiskers.*)

RABBIT: I'm a real rabbit.

CONJURER: Of course you are. Come along out of that hat.
(*The rabbit appears to give a jump and come out at the back of the hat. He goes up to the Conjurer and makes such a fuss of him that he is almost overwhelmed. The Conjurer struggles and at length manages to push the rabbit away.*)
That is quite enough of that. Go and stand over there. (*He points to a place at the side, and the rabbit obeys.*)
I shall now make more magic. I shall make smoke without fire. (*He waves his wand over hat.*)
Rappity frappity come up smoke. (*Smoke comes up which is made from a lighted cigarette below.*)
I have one last piece of magic. (*He waves his wand over the stage and from below rise coloured bubbles. (These are made*

from material that can be bought from any trick shop.) The rabbit, uttering cries of delight, jumps about trying to catch the bubbles.)

(To audience) : Thank you for your kind attention.

CURTAIN DOWN

CURTAIN UP

ACT FIVE

(Enter a puppet with very full trousers, carrying beads on a string.)

BAGGY PANTS : I'm called Baggy Pants because I wear baggy trousers. You must now meet my two performing pigs. *(Enter Porky and Pinky holding hands, and Baggy Pants brings them to the front and they bow to the audience.)*

BAGGY PANTS : These pigs are very clever. They are the only pigs in the world who can count. Pinky, take hold of the other end of this bead string. *(Pinky does so and the bead string with the five beads is stretched between them.)*

BAGGY PANTS : Now, Porky, count the beads.

(Porky goes behind the beads and touching each bead says) :

PORKY : One, two, three, four, twenty.

BAGGY PANTS : That's not right. *(He turns to audience.)* I am so sorry. Try again, Porky.

PORKY : One, two, three, four, ten.

BAGGY PANTS : You are doing it on purpose. Pinky, fetch my big stick and I'll soon show him how to count. *(Pinky goes off and returns with the stick, which, however, she gives to Porky.)*

PORKY : I'm sick and tired of this act, and I'm going to teach *you* a lesson.

(He begins to belabour Baggy Pants, at the same time crying) One, two, three, four, five. One, two, three, four, five. One, two, three, four, five. *(Baggy Pants runs round the stage chased by Porky and Pinky, and Baggy Pants crying for help. Enter the Ringmaster.)*

RINGMASTER : What is going on here? You can't behave like this even if it is a rehearsal. *(Chasing stops.)* You can all go home

The Circus Rehearsal

and if your act isn't better tomorrow I shall sack you. (*Exeunt Baggy Pants and the Pigs.*)
(*To audience*) : That was shocking! However, I shall control the next act myself. You shall see Horace, my Wonder Horse, and Sylvia, the beautiful rider.
(*Sylvia enters leading the horse. They come centre and both bow to the audience. Horse stays front but Sylvia goes to the back of the stage.
Ringmaster fetches the 3 in. cube and puts it on the playing board.*)
(*To Horace*) : Stand on your back legs.
(*With a flourish Horace flings up his front legs and puts them on to the cube.*)
Down, Horace, down. (*Horace jumps down.*)
Dance, Horace, dance. (*Horace dances.*)
Stop, Horace. (*Horace stops.*)
Go to sleep, Horace. (*Horace puts his head on to the cube.*)
Up, Horace, up. (*Horace gets up.*)
(*Ringmaster pats Horace.*)
Sylvia, bring him his sugar.
(*Sylvia comes over to Horace and holds something to his mouth. Sylvia makes a fuss of Horace and he reciprocates.*)
Are you both ready to ride?
Sylvia : Yes, we are ready.
(*The horse stands sideways to the stage and Sylvia jumps on to his back. Actually Sylvia is only standing at the side of the horse, but her full skirt spreads over the horse's back and she appears to be riding. They walk, trot, and gallop. Horace goes backwards as well as forwards.*)
Ringmaster : Now for your famous ride.
(*Sylvia and Horace go to one end of the stage and when riding Sylvia seems to fall over and under the horse as he trots, and then she returns to an upright riding position. She repeats this and then jumps off the horse.*)
That was excellent. (*He pats Horace.*) (*Calls.*) All on for the final act.
(*Enter all the puppets who walk round the stage. They stand still with the Ringmaster centre.*)

CURTAIN DOWN

XI: *The Kitten who Wanted to Purr*

CHARACTERS

Kitten
Rabbit
Three Bears
Fox

Santa Claus or
    Father Christmas
Boy
Girl

PROPERTIES

Tree
Log
Sleigh loaded with parcels

CURTAIN UP

SCENE ONE

Country winter scene.

(*A rabbit hops in. He stops to rub his whiskers.*)
RABBIT: Goodness, my whiskers are cold. I must hurry home or they will get frozen to my face.
(*He hears "mew, mew, mew", coming from behind the tree.*)
I don't like the sound of that. It's no one I know. I think I'll hurry on.
(*The mewing is repeated. Rabbit very cautiously goes towards the tree and the mewing stops. He turns to go home and the crying continues. Rabbit goes slowly up to tree and looks behind it, and at the same time a very small kitten puts its head round and comes to the front.*)
KITTEN: Mew, mew, mew.
RABBIT: So it's you who was crying. What's the matter with you?
KITTEN: I don't know where I am and I'm so cold.
(*She rubs her paws together.*)
RABBIT: Jump on to this log and let me look at you.

(*Kitten scrambles on to the log which is on the playing board.*)
You are very small to be out alone. I'll help you to find your way home.

KITTEN: Oh thank you, but I haven't got a home. (*Cries again.*)

RABBIT: What, no home!

KITTEN: I used to have a lovely one with my mother and brothers and sisters in a shed, but the wind blew the shed over. Mother told us all to run, but I must have run the wrong way for I haven't seen any of the others since it happened. (*Begins to cry.*) Now I'm lost.

RABBIT (*He goes up to the kitten and gently strokes her*): That is very sad. What are you going to do?

KITTEN: Well, I thought I might try to be a Christmas present.

RABBIT: A Christmas present! What kind of an animal is that?

KITTEN: It's not an animal. My grandmother was one when she was little. She said you have someone to love you, and you learn to purr.

RABBIT: That sounds good. What do you mean by purr?

KITTEN: You make a sound like a bee. I've tried but I can't do it.

RABBIT: Let me hear you.

(*Kitten tries to purr, but only makes a most peculiar sound. Rabbit hops about and around laughing heartily at the sound. He stops by Kitten.*)

You had better come to my home, while it's so cold, and I'll look after you. (*He takes Kitten by the hand and they begin to go off stage. A fox enters and calls to them.*)

FOX: Hello, where are you two going?

RABBIT: This kitten wants to be a Christmas present. Do you know about such things?

FOX: I know that tomorrow is the day of Christmas presents.

RABBIT: Hooray, who told you that?

FOX: The three bears told me today. They know because Santa Claus brings them presents each year.

RABBIT: Can you take us to the bears?

FOX: Yes, I'll help you if you can come now before it gets dark. (*Exeunt, the rabbit hopping, the fox running and the kitten keeping close to the rabbit.*)

CURTAIN DOWN

CURTAIN UP

SCENE TWO

Entrance to a cave.

(Enter Fox, Rabbit and Kitten. They knock at the entrance of the cave. A voice from within says "Who is it?")

Fox: It's Fox. Can you help some friends of mine?

(Three Bears come out of the cave.)

1st Bear: What do you want?

Fox: This kitten wants to be a Christmas present, and I thought that you could tell her all about them.

1st Bear: Why do you want to be one?

Kitten: If I am a Christmas present someone will love me and I shall learn how to purr.

2nd Bear: Can't you purr?

Rabbit: Show them what you can do.

(Kitten makes her funny noise and all the animals are doubled up with laughter.)

2nd Bear: Please stop that noise, otherwise I shall never do anything. *(Kitten stops.)*

3rd Bear: I think we should try to help her. *(He turns to the kitten.)* Father Christmas will be passing here very soon.

Kitten: Can I wait to see him?

3rd Bear: You must not see him fill our stockings. He wouldn't like that, but you can wait for him by the road. Come over here. *(Bear takes Kitten to side front of stage.)*

1st Bear *(walking up to Kitten)*: This is where his sleigh will pass.

2nd Bear: Let us line up across the road so that he will not miss us.

(The animals hold paws to make a line. There is a sound of bells and galloping off stage, and then a sleigh comes along the playing shelf. (This is moved from below.) Santa Claus is at the front of the sleigh.)

Santa Claus: Whoa, whoa. *(Sleigh stops and Santa Claus jumps from the sleigh.)* Why are all you animals out? You should be thinking of going to bed.

1st Bear: Please, Santa Claus, this little kitten is very unhappy. She is all alone and she wants to be a Christmas present.

The Kitten who Wanted to Purr

Kitten (*coming up to Father Christmas and holding up her paws*): Dear Father Christmas, please, please help me.
Santa Claus: Bless your heart, you shall be a Christmas present. I know the very home to take you to. Jump on my sleigh at the back. (*Kitten gets on sleigh as directed and Father Christmas turns to the animals.*)
You animals have been very kind and good, and I promise you that I will look after your kitten. Now all of you hurry home. (*Santa Claus gets on to his sleigh.*)
Kitten: Good-bye, animals. I'll never forget you.
(*Sleigh begins to move off stage. Kitten waves her paw and all the animals call out good-bye.*)

CURTAIN DOWN

CURTAIN UP

SCENE THREE

The interior of a room. A Christmas tree is on the playing board (or top shelf) and curled up beside it is the kitten.
(*Enter a boy and a girl.*)
Boy: Let's go and look at the Christmas tree.
(*They walk towards the tree and begin to look at it and the kitten remains fast asleep.*)
Girl: Oh, look at this darling little kitten.
(*Kitten begins to wake up and stretches herself. Girl goes up to her and begins to hug her.*)
You must be my Christmas present. I love you, I love you.
(*Continues to fuss kitten.*)
Boy: She may be hungry. I'll go and get her some milk.
(*Exit Boy, who returns almost immediately with a bowl of milk which he puts on to the playing board.*)
Girl: Come and drink this milk, Kitty.
(*Kitten goes to the milk and drinks. When she has finished she looks at the audience and begins to purr loudly and correctly. She then goes to the Girl and gets as close to her as possible. Boy comes to Kitten and strokes her. Kitten begins to purr again.*)

CURTAIN DOWN

XII: The Cat who was Lonely

A glove puppet play for the little ones.

CHARACTERS

CAT
PIG
DUCK

CROW
COCK
MOUSE

CURTAIN UP

SCENE

Any scene with an exterior of a house.

CAT (*the cat is outside her house crying*): Mew, mew, mew. (*Walks up and down.*) I'm so lonely. (*Puts paws to face and cries. Enter Pig.*)
PIG: Good morning, Cat.
CAT: Good morning, Pig.
PIG: Why are you crying, little Cat?
CAT: Because I am lonely.
PIG: I am lonely too. Let us live together in your beautiful house.
CAT: You want to live with me?
PIG: Yes, yes, yes.
CAT: First I must hear you sing.
PIG: I sing nicely. My piggies love to hear me. Grunt, grunt, grunt. I've got a lovely voice. Grunt, grunt, grunt. (*Goes on grunting until Cat puts her paws to ears.*)
CAT: Please stop singing, Pig, for I do not like your voice. I would rather live alone, so please go away. (*Exit Pig very crossly. Cat cries again. Enter Hen.*)
HEN: Good morning, Cat.
CAT: Good morning, Hen.
HEN: Why are you crying, little Cat?
CAT: Because I am lonely.

The Cat who was Lonely

HEN: I am lonely too. Let us live together in your beautiful house.
CAT: Are you sure you want to live with me?
HEN: Yes, yes, yes.
CAT: First I must hear you sing.
HEN: My chicks love to hear me sing. Cluck, cluck, cluck. I've got a lovely voice. Cluck, cluck, cluck. (*Goes on clucking until Cat puts her paws to ears.*)
CAT: Please stop singing, Hen, for I do not like your voice. I would rather live alone, so please go away. (*Exit Hen crossly. Cat cries again. Enter Duck.*)

The same dialogue and actions continue with each animal except that the

Duck sings Quack, quack, quack.
Crow sings Caw, caw, caw.
Cock sings Cock-a-doodle-doo, cock-a-doodle-doo.
(*Exit Cock crossly. Cat cries again. Enter Mouse.*)

MOUSE: Good morning, Cat.
CAT: Good morning, Mouse.
MOUSE: Why are you crying, Cat.
CAT: Because I am lonely.
MOUSE: I am lonely too. Let us live together in your beautiful house.
CAT: Are you sure you want to live with me?
MOUSE: Yes, yes, yes.
CAT: First I must hear you sing.
MOUSE: I sing sweetly, everyone says so. Quee, quee, quee. My voice is soft. Quee, quee, quee. (*Goes on queeing until Cat interrupts.*)
CAT: Your voice is lovely. I should love you to live with me.
(*Exeunt Cat and Mouse into house.*)

CURTAIN DOWN

XIII: The Three Little Pigs

A glove puppet play.

CHARACTERS

Mother Pig
Spotty
Pinky

Curly
Wolf

CURTAIN UP

SCENE ONE

Inside the Mother Pig's house.

Mother Pig: My darling little pigs, you are now four months old, and it is time for you to go out into the world and take care of yourselves. I cannot keep you here any longer.

Spotty: If we leave who will do your dusting, sweeping and cooking?

Mother Pig: I shall have to do it myself.

Pinky: I don't want to leave you, Mother.

Mother Pig: Dear Pinky, I shall miss you, but it is right that you should go.

Curly: Where shall we live?

Mother Pig: A very sensible question, Curly. I shall help each of you to build a little house and then you must manage on your own.

Spotty (*He jumps up and down in an excited sort of way*): I should like a house of straw, for straw is so warm and soft. Please may I have a house of straw?

Mother Pig: I should be able to manage that, Spotty. What sort of a house do you want, Pinky?

Pinky (*She goes up to her mother and puts her trotters round her*): If I must go I should like a house of sticks. I could put curtains up at the windows and have flowers growing outside.

The Three Little Pigs

MOTHER PIG: That would look very nice. Now, Curly, tell me about your house?
CURLY (*He walks up and down all the time he is talking*): I want a house made of bricks, to keep out the sun in summer and the snow in winter.
MOTHER PIG: You are very clever piggies and I am proud of you. You shall each have the kind of house you want.
THREE PIGS (*They hold trotters and dance*): Hurrah, hurrah, we're going to have our own little houses.
MOTHER PIG: Let us go and build the houses.
(*Exeunt Pigs.*)

CURTAIN DOWN

CURTAIN UP

SCENE TWO

The straw house. The house can be made with three sides of a box placed on the playing board, with the fourth side, facing the back, cut away. The house should be covered with straw and there should be a window and a door.

(*Spotty and his mother come out of the house.*)
MOTHER PIG: Your house is now finished and you should be very comfortable. I want you to remember two things, so listen carefully.
SPOTTY: Yes, Mother.
MOTHER PIG: First about your spots. Remember to wash them every day.
SPOTTY: Yes, Mother.
MOTHER PIG: Now about the Wolf. He will tell you that he is a friend, but you must take no notice, for he only wants to eat you.
SPOTTY: I'll be careful and I will not listen to a word that he says.
MOTHER PIG: Very well. Now I shall leave you.
(*Mother kisses Spotty and goes. Spotty goes into the house and comes out almost immediately holding a little broom. He proceeds to sweep all along the playing board. He goes into the house and can be heard singing inside.
Enter Wolf.*)

WOLF: This is a new house and I can hear someone singing. I think I can smell pig and I'd like to find out. (*He knocks at the door.*)
SPOTTY: Who is knocking at my door?
WOLF: A friend.
(*Spotty looks out of the window.*)
SPOTTY: I can see a wolf and you are no friend of mine.
WOLF: Let me in, little pig.
SPOTTY: No, by the hair of my chinny chin chin, I will not let you in.
WOLF: Then I'll huff and I'll puff and I'll blow your house down.
SPOTTY: You may try but it won't be of any use.
(*Wolf huffs and puffs and as he does so he goes up to the house and knocks it off the playing board. Spotty comes out of the house, shouting.*)
Help, help, the Wolf is after me. (*He runs off, followed by the Wolf.*)

CURTAIN DOWN

CURTAIN UP

SCENE THREE

The House of Sticks. The house should be made in the same way as the straw house, but it should be covered with sticks. There are curtains at the windows and flowers at the side.
(*Pinky and her mother come out of the house.*)
MOTHER PIG: You have a very pretty house, Pinky, and you should be happy here. I want you to listen carefully to what I have to say.
PINKY: Yes, Mother.
MOTHER PIG: First about the flowers. You must remember to water them every day.
PINKY: Yes, Mother.
MOTHER PIG: Now about the Wolf. He will tell you that he is a friend, but you must take no notice for he only wants to eat you.
PINKY: I'll be careful and I won't open the door.
MOTHER PIG: You should be safe, so I will leave you to live

The Three Little Pigs

alone. (*Mother kisses Pinky and goes. Pinky goes into the house and comes out again almost immediately, holding a watering can. She waters her flowers and then returns to the house and can be heard singing inside.*
Enter Wolf.)
WOLF: Here is a new house, and someone is living in it, for I can hear her singing. If there is a pig inside I must not frighten her. (*He knocks at the door.*)
PINKY: Who is knocking at my door?
WOLF (*He turns to the audience and says*): I lost the pig who lived in the straw house, so I must be careful. (*He turns towards the house again.*) I am a friend, so please open the door and let me in.
(*Pinky looks out of the window.*)
PINKY: You are the Wolf and my mother told me not to listen to you. Go away.
WOLF: I'm really very kind. Let me come in.
PINKY: No, by the hair on my chinny chin chin, I will not let you in.
WOLF: Then I'll huff and I'll puff and I'll blow your house down.
PINKY: You can huff and you can puff but you won't blow my house down.
(*Wolf huffs and puffs and going up to the house, while huffing and puffing, he knocks it off the playing board. Pinky comes out of the house shouting.*)
You won't catch me for I know where to hide.
(*She runs off followed by Wolf.*)

CURTAIN DOWN

CURTAIN UP

SCENE FOUR

The brick house. The house is constructed in the same way as the others, but it also has a chimney on the roof cut away at the back similarly to the house. It is painted to represent bricks.
(*Curly and his mother come from the back of the house.*)
MOTHER PIG: Your house looks very nice indeed. Now listen carefully to what I have to say.

CURLY: Yes, Mother.

MOTHER PIG: Remember to curl your tail every day.

CURLY: Yes, Mother.

MOTHER PIG: I quite expect the Wolf to call, and he will say that he is my friend. This is not true, for he only wishes to eat you, so do not open the door to him.

CURLY: I will try to be careful.

MOTHER PIG: Good-bye, Curly, for I must leave you now.

(*Exit Mother Pig. Curly goes into his house, and he returns almost immediately holding a mat which he shakes. He then holds it up to the audience so that they can see the word* "Welcome" *written on it. He returns to the house and can be heard singing.*
Enter the Wolf.)

WOLF: This looks like another pig's house, so I may as well try and get in. (*He knocks at the door.*)

CURLY: Who is knocking at my door?

WOLF: It's a dear friend of your mother's. Your house is so delightful outside, that I should like to see the inside. (*Curly looks out of the window.*)

CURLY: You think you are very clever, but I know that you are the Wolf and I shall certainly not let you in.

WOLF: Yes, I am the Wolf, and you must open the door.

CURLY: No, by the hair of my chinny chin chin, I will not let you in.

WOLF: Then I'll huff and I'll puff and I'll blow your house down.

(*The Wolf huffs and puffs, and huffs and puffs until he is tired, but he cannot blow the house down.*)

CURLY: Ha, ha, ha. You are not as clever as you thought you were.

WOLF (*He walks up and down the front of the stage saying*): I'm very angry. I'll get into his house somehow. (*He turns to the audience.*) I know what I'll do. I'll climb on to the roof and get down the chimney. (*Curly watches the Wolf all the time from the window.*

The Wolf goes to the back of the house and his head slowly appears at the top of the roof. He puts his head close to the chimney; and then with a quick twist of the wrist the puppeteer brings the puppet head down into the chimney so that it appears that the Wolf has fallen down the chimney.

During these actions Curly makes frequent appearances at the window, telling the audience the progress that the Wolf is making. When the Wolf reaches the top of the house

CURLY (*to the audience*): The Wolf is coming down the chimney soon, but he is going to get a big surprise, for I have put a big pot of water on the fire and when he comes down the chimney he will fall into it.

(*There is a loud clatter and bang.*)

I must look inside because the Wolf seems to have fallen into my pot. (*He leaves window and goes into house. He comes out of the house.*) That's the end of the horrid old Wolf. Mother will be pleased. (*He begins to dance up and down the stage. Enter Spotty and Pinky.*)

SPOTTY: Did we hear you say that the old Wolf won't trouble us any more?

CURLY: Yes, go and look at him inside the house.

(*Spotty and Pinky go into the house while Curly continues to dance. Spotty and Pinky return and Pinky hugs Curly.*)

PINKY: You are a clever pig.

(*The three pigs join trotters and dance.*)

CURTAIN DOWN

XIV: The Queen of Hearts—Nursery Rhyme

The idea of this story came from children.

CHARACTERS

Knave	Queen
Cook	King
Susan the Kitchen Maid	Attendant

PROPERTIES

Basin
Tray on which there are six pastry tart cases
Apron. If a wire is threaded through the top hem it will fix round the Queen without any fastenings
Cup
Stick

CURTAIN UP

SCENE ONE

Inside a kitchen.

(*Enter Knave. He looks carefully all round.*)
Knave: Good, no one is here. I'll see what I can find to eat. (*He looks all round again, and eventually stops before some jars on the playing shelf.*) Plum jam! Rice! Flour! I don't want those. Ah, what is this? (*He holds up a jar of a yellow colour.*) It's a pretty colour. I think I'll try it. (*He tries it.*) Oh-h-h. It is mustard. (*Coughs.*)
(*Enter the Cook and Susan.*)
Cook (*to Knave*): Whatever is the matter with you?
(*The Knave is coughing too much to answer, and he goes out.*) Today is very important, for the Queen is coming to visit my kitchen, and she is certain to want to do some cooking. Bring a basin to me, Susan, and don't drop it.

The Queen of Hearts

(*Susan gets a basin, brings it over to the Cook, and then drops it. There is a sound of breaking crockery as it falls.*)
You are a naughty girl.
SUSAN: Why did you say don't drop it? You made me nervous. (*She cries loudly.*)
COOK: Stop that noise and fetch the pastry that I made this morning. (*Exit Susan, who returns carrying some tarts without jam on a tray.*) Put them here (*Susan puts them on to the playing shelf*) and now go and clear up the broken china. (*Exit Susan.*)
I hope the Queen will like this pastry.
(*Enter the Queen.*)
QUEEN: Your kitchen looks very nice, Cook.
COOK: Thank you, Your Majesty.
QUEEN: I should like to make some tarts.
COOK: Certainly, Your Majesty. Everything is ready.
QUEEN: Bring my apron. (*Cook fetches the apron and puts it round the Queen.*) Thank you, Cook. Now bring me the jam. (*Cook brings a pot of jam clearly marked "plum".*)
This is plum jam, Cook.
COOK: Yes, Your Majesty.
QUEEN: But the King likes strawberry jam. Please take this away and bring me strawberry.
(*Cook takes away the plum jam and brings back a dish of strawberry jam.*)
Sometimes I think cooking gets more difficult every time I do it. (*She puts a spoon into the jam and fills the pastry cases.*)
They really look delicious. The King loves my cooking.
(*Enter the Knave, still coughing.*)
Whatever is the matter, Knave?
KNAVE: I may have a crumb in my throat.
QUEEN: Can you give him a drink, Cook?
COOK (*to Knave*): Have you been eating mustard?
QUEEN (*laughing*): Now, Cook, don't tease. Why should he eat mustard?
(*Cook goes and fetches a cup of water which the Knave takes and drinks.*)
KNAVE: That makes me feel better.
QUEEN: Now I have made the tarts I must go. You had better come with me, Knave. (*Exeunt Queen and Knave. Enter Susan.*)

Cook: I'm going to put these tarts in the oven. (*Cooks takes tarts.*) Clear up while I am away. (*Exit Cook with the tarts. Susan goes to the strawberry jam, dips her finger into it and puts it to her mouth. She repeats this two or three times. She then picks up the dish and drops it. Sound of broken glass. Cook hurries in.*)
What have you done?
Susan: I've dropped the jam. (*She begins to cry loudly.*)
Cook: Stop that noise and clear up the mess.

CURTAIN DOWN

CURTAIN UP

SCENE TWO

A palace room. Knave is fast asleep.

(*Enter the Cook carrying the tarts. She puts them on to the playing board and goes out. Knave wakes up, slowly stretches and walks front. He sees the tarts.*)
Knave: Oh, what beautiful tarts. (*He walks away from them and returns.*) Oh, what beautiful tarts. (*He walks away but returns.*) These tarts are for the King, so I must not touch them. (*He walks away but returns.*) I'll just eat one, but no one must see me. I'll take the tarts behind the curtain. (*He picks up the tarts and takes them behind the curtain.*
Enter the Queen and the King with an Attendant.)
Queen: I've had such a busy morning. I've been making some tarts for you.
King: My dear Queen, I am longing to eat one of your tarts. You are such a good cook.
Queen: You flatter me. Nevertheless I seldom have a failure. If you like to call for them you can have them to eat now.
King (*calls*): Bring in the tarts made by Her Majesty.
Cook (*Cook enters and bows to the King*): Your Majesty, did you call for the Queen's tarts?
King: Certainly I did.
Cook: I put the tarts on that shelf. (*Points to the place where she left them.*)

The Queen of Hearts

KING: They are not there now. You must find them.
(*Sounds of groans from behind the curtain.*)
QUEEN: What is that noise?
KING (*to Attendant*): Go and look behind the curtain.
(*Attendant goes to curtain.*)
ATTENDANT: It's the Knave, Your Majesty.
(*Knave comes from the curtain holding his stomach.*)
QUEEN: What is the matter, Knave?
KNAVE: I don't feel very well.
(*Cook goes over to him.*)
COOK: Do you feel sick? (*Knave nods.*) First you eat mustard and now I think that you have eaten tarts.
KING: Tell me, where are the tarts?
KNAVE: Perhaps the cat has eaten them.
QUEEN: Don't be so silly, Knave.
KING: I am getting very angry, and I order you to tell me. Have you eaten the Queen's tarts?
QUEEN: Tell us the truth, Knave.
KNAVE (*He goes to the King and bends low*): I took the tarts.
KING: Rascal! Have you eaten them?
KNAVE: Most of them, our Majesty.
KING: How many are left?
KNAVE: One, Your Majesty.
COOK: I'm not surprised that he feels sick.
KING: Go and fetch the one tart that is left.
(*Knave goes to the curtain and returns with tray on which there is one tart.*)
Put it on the shelf. I will eat it after I've dealt with you.
(*Knave puts tray back on to the playing board.*)
QUEEN (*to Cook*): You may go back to the kitchen, Cook.
KING (*to Knave*): I am going to teach you a lesson so that next time you feel greedy you will remember this punishment.
(*To Attendant*): Fetch me a stick. (*Exit Attendant.*)
(*To Knave*): Have you anything to say?
KNAVE: I am very, very sorry, Your Majesty.
QUEEN: I am sure that he is really sorry. Can't you forgive him?
(*Attendant returns with stick. King takes the stick.*)
KING (*to Attendant*): You may go. (*Exit Attendant.*)
(*To Knave*): How many tarts did you eat?
KNAVE: Five, Your Majesty.
KING: Then I shall beat you twice for every tart you stole.

QUEEN: That is far too many. I will make you some more tarts.
KING: Very well, I'll make it five. You had better go, my dear.
(*Exit Queen.*)
(*To Knave*): I shall beat you full sore. Turn round, Knave.
(*Knave turns front and King beats him five times.*)
KNAVE: Oh, oh, oh, oh, oh. I will never, never touch anything again.

CURTAIN DOWN

XV: Mrs. Popple and her Pet Goose

A shadow play written by children of 6½—7 years with the co-operation of their class teacher

CHARACTERS

STORY TELLER
MRS. POPPLE
AUGUSTUS HER GOOSE
A GOOSE WITH A HURT WING
RABBIT
JENNY WREN
BEE
DONKEY
FOX

The actions of the shadow puppets synchronise with the words of the story.

CURTAIN UP

STORY TELLER (*who stands side front of the stage*): This is the story of Mrs. Popple and her pet goose whose name was Augustus. Mrs. Popple lived in a little house (*pause while a house is placed on the shadow screen*). One morning Mrs. Popple came out of her house (*enter Mrs. Popple*) and called to her goose.
MRS. POPPLE: Augustus, Augustus come here. (*Augustus enters from opposite side of screen.*)
STORY TELLER: Mrs. Popple loved Augustus very much and she gave him plenty to eat and she tried to be his friend, but Augustus was often lonely because he had no geese friends. This morning Mrs. Popple said
MRS. POPPLE: Let us go for a walk. (*As they are walking across the screen a goose with a torn wing flies slowly over them and then flies off.*)
MRS. POPPLE: Look at that poor goose. He is flying very slowly and I think that he has hurt his wing. If he comes down in the

marsh the fox will eat him. (*Mrs. Popple and Augustus enter house. Augustus comes out of the house almost immediately.*)
STORY TELLER: Augustus kept thinking about the goose with the hurt wing and at last he decided to go and look for him.
AUGUSTUS (*calling*): Mrs. Popple, I'm going to look for the hurt goose before the fox gets him. I shan't be long. (*As he is going off a rabbit enters from the opposite direction.*)
RABBIT: Where are you going?
AUGUSTUS: I am going to find the goose with the hurt wing. Have you seen him?
RABBIT: Yes. He was flying very slowly. Shall I come with you?
AUGUSTUS: Yes, please. (*Augustus and Rabbit go off and Jenny Wren enters. Augustus and Rabbit return and meet Jenny Wren.*)
JENNY WREN: Where are you going?
AUGUSTUS: We are going to find the goose with the hurt wing. Have you seen him?
JENNY WREN: Yes. He was flying very slowly. Shall I come with you?
AUGUSTUS: Yes, please. (*Augustus, Rabbit and Jenny Wren go off and Bee enters. Augustus, Rabbit and Jenny Wren return.*)
BEE: Where are you going?
AUGUSTUS: We are going to find the goose with the hurt wing. Have you seen him?
BEE: Yes, he was flying very slowly. Shall I come with you?
AUGUSTUS: Yes, please. (*Augustus, Rabbit, Jenny Wren and Bee go off and Donkey enters. Augustus, Rabbit, Jenny Wren and Bee return.*)
DONKEY: Where are you going?
AUGUSTUS: We are going to find the goose with the hurt wing. Have you seen him?
DONKEY: Yes, he was flying very slowly. I think he will soon fall down. Shall I come with you?
AUGUSTUS: Yes, please. (*Augustus, Rabbit, Jenny Wren, Bee and Donkey go off. They cross the screen twice, following each other in one long line. When the screen is empty the hurt goose flies in and gradually falls to the ground.*)
STORY TELLER: The goose with the broken wing has fallen to the ground, and here comes the fox to eat him up. (*The fox slowly creeps towards the hurt goose while the goose tries to fly out of his way, but he keeps falling to the ground. Suddenly there

is a noise behind the screen as all the animals, making their own noises, enter. *The fox runs away and the animals stand together while Augustus goes up to the hurt goose.*)

AUGUSTUS : Are you badly hurt?

HURT GOOSE : I have been shot in the wing, and I think it is broken. Thank you all for saving me from the fox, for he was going to eat me.

AUGUSTUS : I'll get Mrs. Popple. She will soon make you well. (*Calls.*) Mrs. Popple, Mrs. Popple, Mrs. Popple. (*Mrs. Popple comes out of the house.*)

MRS. POPPLE : What do you want?

AUGUSTUS : We've found the goose with the hurt wing. Can you make him better?

MRS. POPPLE : Of course I can. Let us take him inside the house where I can look at him. (*Mrs. Popple leads the way into the house and all the animals follow her.*)

STORY TELLER : Mrs. Popple mended the hurt wing, but the goose liked living in the house so much that he asked Mrs. Popple if he could stay for ever. So Augustus was never lonely again, because he had a friend.

(*Mrs. Popple followed by the two geese comes out of the house. Other animals enter from other side of screen and meet Mrs. Popple and geese.*)

CURTAIN DOWN

XVI: The Nativity

A Shadow Play.

It is an advantage to joint the limbs and heads of the shadow puppets.

CHARACTERS

An indefinite number of puppets in Eastern dress to represent people on their way to Bethlehem.

MARY
JOSEPH
DONKEY
INNKEEPER
THREE SHEPHERDS
A SHEPHERD BOY

THREE WISE MEN
THREE SERVANTS
CAMELS
BOY
COW
LAMB

Before each scene there should be a Bible reading, and if desired there can be carol singing or music.

BIBLE READING: LUKE 2, verses 1, 3, 4.

SCREEN DARK

SCENE ONE

ON THE WAY TO BETHLEHEM

On one corner of the screen is an inn, and on the other side a shed.

When the screen is lighted people are seen crossing in groups and singly. One man knocks at the inn, and the Innkeeper comes out. The man talks to the Innkeeper, and they both enter the inn. People continue to cross, but at last the screen is empty. Joseph and Mary slowly cross stage. Mary is sitting on a donkey. (It is

The Nativity

an easy feat to suggest riding. The Mary puppet rests behind the donkey puppet, and the two make one shadow.)

Joseph knocks at the door of the inn, and the Innkeeper comes out. The two appear to talk. While this is going on a boy leading a cow crosses the screen and enters the shed. The Innkeeper points to the shed, and Joseph goes to Mary. The Innkeeper leads Joseph and Mary to the shed and they all enter.

SCREEN DARK

BIBLE READING: LUKE 2, verses 8 and 9.

SCENE TWO

THE SHEPHERDS

Shadow of a hill slope—sheep on hill.

SCREEN LIGHT

Enter three shepherds (one alone and two together). They form a group on the slope. (With experiment it is possible to give the impression of sitting.)

The shepherd boy enters and joins the other shepherds.

Quiet music—the music stops.

The Angel Gabriel appears.

The shepherds rise and bow their heads. Verses 10, 11 and 12 of Luke 2 should then be spoken. Angel Gabriel disappears.

Shepherds seem to talk and exeunt with the boy leading.

SCREEN DARK

BIBLE READING: MATTHEW 2, verses 1 and 2.

SCENE THREE

THE WISE MEN

An Eastern scene. Star in sky.

SCREEN LIGHT

First Wise Man enters with his servant. The Wise Man points to the star.

Second Wise Man enters from another direction with servant. The two Wise Men bow to each other and talk.

Third Wise Man enters with his servant from a different direction. He greets the two other Wise Men and they all look at the star. The three servants stand in a group together.

SCREEN DARK

BIBLE READING: LUKE 2, verse 15.

SCENE FOUR
SHEPHERDS AND KINGS ON WAY TO THE STABLE

SCREEN LIGHT

Shepherds cross screen, one holding a staff, another a lantern and the boy a lamb. Repeat this crossing to lengthen the scene.

BIBLE READING: MATTHEW 2, verses 9 and 10.

Wise Men cross the screen on camels. Each king can be followed by as many retinue as desired. This scene should be very colourful. Repeat to lengthen.

SCREEN DARK

BIBLE READING: LUKE 2, verses 16, and 17—20.

SCENE FIVE
INSIDE THE STABLE

Outside sit a cow and a donkey. Crib centre with Mary and Joseph on either side.

SCREEN LIGHT

The shepherds enter, and each one in turn goes to the cradle, looks into it and then takes up a position on one side of it.

BIBLE READING: MATTHEW 2, verse 11.

Each Wise Man enters separately and kneels at the crib. Their servants, carrying gifts, stand at the side. After worshipping the Wise Men take up positions round Mary, Joseph and the Baby.

The Nativity

Gabriel takes up a position high above the Holy Family, and during this tableau there is the last BIBLE READING: LUKE 2, verse **19**.

SCREEN DARK

SUGGESTED CAROLS

Scene One	All Bethlehem lay sleeping.
	In a stable poor in Bethlehem.
Scene Two	While shepherds watched their flocks by night.
	Shepherds, shake off your drowsy sleep.
Scene Three	We Three Kings of Orient are.
	The First Nowell.
Scene Four	Mary had a little Baby.
	Holy Night.
Scene Five	Away in a Manger.
	Good Christian men rejoice.

XVII: Peter and the Wolf as a Shadow Play

CHARACTERS

PETER
GRANDFATHER
WOLF

BIRD
DUCK
CAT

PROPERTIES

A gramophone record of *Peter and the Wolf*. The story of *Peter and the Wolf* from the book by Sergei Prokofiev.

Anyone producing this play will want to decide for himself which sections of the music he will use during the play.

The reader of the story can sit (in view, or out of view of the audience) when he reads the book. All conversations should be said by the children manipulating the puppets.

The movements of the puppets should synchronise with the descriptive readings. For example, "seeing the duck, the little bird flew down upon the grass and settled next to her". The business of lassoing the wolf can be made to look realistic, and the rope made to catch the wolf's tail quite successfully.

No further details of this production are given, for it is essentially an individual creation, and one that can be most successfully produced.